Family Kitchen

One Yummy Mummy

Family Kitchen

Jolene Cox

ORPEN PRESS

Published by
Orpen Press
Upper Floor, Unit B3
Hume Centre
Hume Avenue
Park West Industrial Estate
Dublin 12

email: info@orpenpress.com

www.orpenpress.com

© Jolene Cox, 2021

ISBN: 978-178605-157-8

Printed in Malta by Gutenberg Press Ltd.

Thank You

I have to start with my two peas in a pod, Damien and Lily Mae. Thank you for believing in this dream just as much as me.

Lily Mae, my only hope is I live up to how good you really think I am. You make me burst with pride every day and I am so lucky to have you by my side, cracking the eggs and with your beautiful infectious smile. Never change my girlie.

To my Damien, the one who's in my corner cheering me on, celebrating the highs but also guiding and helping me overcome the lows of this crazy rollercoaster. My calm in a crisis, your sound practical advice is always exactly what is needed. You are the one in the background, helping and supporting me at cooking demos. Myself and Lils, 'your girlies', are so lucky to have you, keeping the show on the road. You never ask for credit; you deserve so much.

To our extended family:

My sister Michelle who listens to me bang on about the obstacle I'm trying to get over in any given week without judgement. Not only did you help us decide on the final cover, you are a deal-maker in so many decisions behind the scenes.

Mammy and Brian for always supporting me and telling me to keep trucking on.

Thank you, Tom and Therese (the real foodies), Brian and Sitha, and Paddy and Linda.

To the Coxes:

Jimmy, my father-in-law, Lily Mae's grandad, for all your fantastic love and support.

Derek and Caroline, for every like on every Facebook post that I've ever posted from day one (that's a lot of likes!).

Sharon for the chats and Mike for all the help with my business plan and projections.

My best friend, Louise, a total rock star. I am so proud to call you a friend, thank you for your loyalty always.

Gerry and Fiona at Orpen Press for putting a punt on me yet again, for allowing me to just be myself. To Eileen for your amazing editing, I know you had your work cut out with me.

Benil for the whole vision and design of this and all your patience, especially with Chapter 8!

To Simon (and Auds) for capturing all those special cooking moments on camera I now can cherish with Lils.

Frankie for not only being my agent but listening and guiding me through the stuff that goes over my head!

To Jenny Cox for finding the words I can never find and for being on the end of the phone always when I need it. I would be so lost without you!

To Jen Hogan for understanding this crazy online world we live in; I'm so lucky we are real friends for life.

Sue for the calm when I need it! Breda, one of my oldest friends, the biggest Fermanagh PR machine a girl could hope for.

Contents

Happiness is children eating their food no matter what.

Hey lovelies,

Welcome back to the One Yummy Mummy kitchen and this, my second cookbook on family cooking, designed to take the stress and strain out of mealtimes and put the fun back in!

Have you ever walked into the kitchen, opened presses full of ingredients while shouts come from another room, "What's for dinner?", and thought, "I actually don't know!"

As a mother, I understand that cooking the main evening meal can be the most stressful time of the day, leaving you feeling totally uninspired. But, with the right recipes up our sleeves, we can make home-cooking easy, accessible and fun. And this is what lies at the heart of *One Yummy Mummy: Family Kitchen* – a space for you to enjoy new recipes and be part of our growing cooking community.

For the past twenty years I have been developing and perfecting family recipes designed to take the hassle out of everyday cooking. I believe that the heart of the home lies firmly in the kitchen, and I am passionate about encouraging kids to get hands-on with cooking that will excite and inspire their taste buds and teach them skills for life.

Over the last five years, I have pioneered a home-cooking movement across the nation by founding the Homecooks Ireland Facebook group, initiating a school's cookery programme for parents, hosting summer cooking camps for kids, giving online cooking workshops and launching my first cookbook, *One Yummy Mummy: Family Food Made Easy*, which thanks to you guys is a bestseller!

So, come on this cooking adventure with us! Parent to parent – from my kitchen to yours.

Jolene and Lils x

Message from Lils:
I hope you enjoy cooking recipes from our new cookbook. Don't forget to send us a pic of your cooking creations!

Come find us:
Join our Family Cooking Club: www.oneyummymummy.com
Instagram: @oneyummymummy1
Facebook: @oneyummymummy1
Twitter: @oneyummymummy1

Hey lovelies, I wanted to write a quick few lines about Chapter 8, Kids in the Kitchen, and what it means to me.

As a busy mother, I completely understand that the idea of letting kids into the kitchen to do the cooking may very well be a living nightmare! There can be visions of a crime-scene-type clean-up operation, along with the added pressure of a wrestling match over who gets to lick the wooden spoon first.

I have always believed that cooking with kids can be so much more than just making cupcakes and licking the bowl. Getting them involved in the food prep of everyday meals from a young age not only teaches them about ingredients and where our food comes from, it also gives them life skills that they will have well beyond leaving our nest.

The key to getting kids into the kitchen is to give them little jobs that are age appropriate – little things they will enjoy doing, making it a fun, learning atmosphere at home. In my own experience, kids can help at any age with kitchen prep and little jobs like peeling garlic and onions, tearing lettuce for a salad, slicing mushrooms, weighing and adding ingredients, assembling pizza toppings, or egg-washing pastry.

As children grow, they will develop the skills, attention span, and interest in doing bigger cooking jobs, like chopping under adult supervision, paving the way for them to learn essential skills for life.

Since the release of my first cookbook, *One Yummy Mummy: Family Food Made Easy*, I have received so many messages from kids who send Lils and myself photos of their cooking creations every day. So, we felt compelled to dedicate a chapter in *Family Kitchen* just for you. Every single recipe in Chapter 8, Kids in the Kitchen, has been especially developed with you in mind, in a bright, colourful easy-to-read style. These are recipes children not only can cook but will devour.

Sometimes it's not just about the recipes and the ingredients, it's the memories that last a lifetime.

We really hope you guys love it.

Jolene and Lils x

Chapter One

Winner Winner Chicken Dinner

Top tip: Strain the juices off the chicken to make a delicious herby gravy. Place over a medium heat in a saucepan, add 300mls stock and thicken with a cornflour paste.

Whole roast chicken in garlic herby butter

Press to plate

1 hour, 50 minutes

Nothing beats a traditional roast chicken dinner – well, nothing except a fresh herb and garlic roast chicken dinner! So tasty, with all your favourite trimmings or just as it is with simple buttered baguettes, you choose.

INGREDIENTS

1.5 kg free-range chicken

100g unsalted butter, melted

Salt and freshly ground pepper, to taste

2 tbsp freshly chopped parsley

3 sprigs of fresh rosemary

3 sprigs of fresh thyme

4 garlic cloves, crushed

Make a bouquet garni by tying together fresh sprigs of rosemary, parsley and thyme and place them into the cavity of the bird

METHOD

- Preheat oven to 180°C fan.
- Line a deep baking tray with a lid with greaseproof paper.
- Chop herbs, mix with butter and melt over a gentle heat.
- Add the chicken to your baking tray.
- Brush your chicken with the herby melted butter, completely covering your bird, reserving a little butter for the end.
- Place a bouquet garni into the cavity of the bird and put on the lid.
- Oven bake for 1 hour, 20 minutes without checking. It's important not to check the bird as opening the door will cool down the heat circulating in the oven.
- After the allocated time, take the lid off and brush the chicken with reserved butter.
- Put your chicken back in without the lid for 20 minutes to let the skin crisp up.
- When crisp, check by piercing beside the leg with a knife to check that the juice runs clear.
- Leave to rest for 5 minutes before carving.
- A perfect roast chicken that really packs a flavour punch.

Top tip: You can also use fresh cod or hake – no need to bash those with the rolling pin though!

Homemade southern-style chicken fillet

The chicken fillet burger is always a popular choice on the menu of any gastronomical dining experience. Tossed in seven not-so-secret spices, flash-fried for five minutes on each side, and topped with our epic homemade burger sauce.

INGREDIENTS

1 chicken breast per person
1 tbsp vegetable oil (plus a drizzle more for frying)
100g cornflour/corn starch
1 tsp each of:
- Paprika
- Smoked paprika
- Salt
- Pepper
- Garlic powder
- Onion powder

A pinch of cayenne pepper

For the burger sauce
2 tbsp mayonnaise
1 tbsp American-style mustard

METHOD

- Bash your chicken breast with a rolling pin to flatten it.
- Mix cornflour and spices together in a shallow dish.
- Brush with oil and toss in the cornflour and spice mix.
- Fry in a well-oiled pan over medium heat for 5 minutes on each side.
- Make your burger sauce and build your burger!
- Epic, home-cooked from scratch and delicious.

Just winging it

Who doesn't love a family wing feast? With delicious sticky barbeque sauce or a spicy, buttery hot sauce, it's finger-licking good! I've given the option here to make your own sauces. By oven-baking your wings, they are healthier than deep frying.

Press to plate

55 minutes

INGREDIENTS

2 tbsp rapeseed oil
800g chicken wing pieces
    (tips removed)

Dry rub
1 tsp smoked paprika
1 tsp paprika
1 tsp onion powder
1 tsp garlic powder
1 tsp black pepper
1 tsp salt

1 tsp dried oregano
A pinch of cayenne pepper
    (watch the heat level)
1 tbsp light soft brown
    sugar

Hot sauce
40g butter, melted
100mls Cayenne pepper
    sauce

Homemade barbeque sauce
4 tbsp tomato ketchup
2 tbsp rice wine vinegar
5 tbsp dark brown sugar
2 tbsp black treacle
    (optional)
2 tbsp honey
1 tbsp Worcestershire sauce
1 tsp Dijon mustard
1 tbsp smoked paprika
Salt and pepper to taste

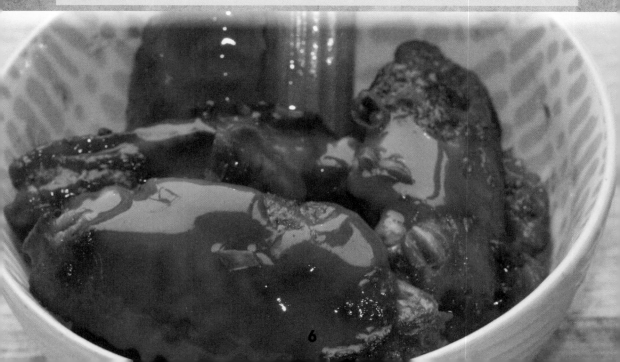

METHOD

- Preheat oven to 180°C fan.
- Pat the wings dry with a kitchen paper towel and add to a large bowl.
- Mix together the oil and dry spices to make your rub and add to the bowl.
- Mix the wings with your hands so they are well covered in the seasoning.
- Arrange chicken wings on a large wire rack on top of a baking sheet lined with greaseproof paper.
- Bake them on the top shelf of your oven for 45 minutes until crispy, turning once halfway through.
- These are delicious wings eaten just baked and seasoned like this for a quick and easy midweek feast.
- Up the flavour game for your family feast by tossing half the wings in hot sauce and the other half in barbeque sauce – you can use shop-bought or make your own.

Hot sauce

- In a small saucepan over gentle heat melt butter with hot sauce and simmer for 10 minutes.

Barbeque sauce

- In a small saucepan over gentle heat mix together the barbeque sauce ingredients until the sugar has dissolved and you are left with a delicious, golden-brown, homemade sticky sauce.

Top tip: Put your wings on a wire rack to bake; this way the heat can circulate around them in the oven, giving you succulent and juicy wings in the middle with a delicious crispy skin.

Top tip: If you are not using leftover chicken, you can cook three chicken breasts in the oven for 30 minutes using the greaseproof paper pouch method on page 66. When cooked, just shred and add to the rest of the ingredients.

Coronation chicken

This classic is a great little recipe for using up any leftover cooked chicken for a picnic or light evening tea. It makes the perfect fresh filling for crusty rolls, wraps or deep-filled baked potatoes.

Press to plate

10 minutes for leftover chicken

Press to plate

40 minutes for fresh chicken breasts

INGREDIENTS

4 cooked diced or shredded chicken breasts
4 tbsp mayonnaise
100g diced cucumber (skin removed)
1 tbsp mango chutney
1 tbsp mild curry powder
100g scallions, snipped
1 tbsp sultanas or dried apricots

METHOD

- In a bowl mix the cooked diced or shredded chicken, mayonnaise, curry powder and mango chutney.
- Add your peeled diced cucumber, sultanas or apricots, and scallions, and give a good mix; season and use in your favourite baked potato or sandwich.

Top tip: Add some fresh chilli and a splash of hot sauce to add some spice.

Creamy tomato, chicken and chorizo pasta

Chorizo and chicken are a match made in heaven in our book. Team them with pasta in a creamy tomato sauce and you are on to a total winner.

INGREDIENTS

400g pasta penne
2 garlic cloves, crushed
½ white onion, diced
1 red pepper, diced
100g chorizo, sliced
4 chicken breasts, diced
1 tbsp dried oregano
1 tsp onion powder
1 tsp garlic powder
½ tsp black pepper
A pinch of salt
200g mascarpone cheese
200g passata
A drizzle of rapeseed oil
Parmesan, to serve

METHOD

- Cook pasta according to packet.
- Over medium heat drizzle some rapeseed oil in a large heavy-based pan.
- Add garlic and onion and fry for 3 minutes until softened
- Scatter the chorizo into the pan and fry for another 2 minutes to release the oils.
- Put in your cubed chicken and cook to seal it for 5 minutes.
- Add red pepper and sprinkle in your oregano and seasoning, mixing as you go.
- Dollop in the mascarpone, letting it melt into a creamy sauce.
- Pour in the passata and give another mix together.
- Finally, drain your cooked penne and add it to the pot.
- Cover and simmer for 5 minutes, making sure the chicken is cooked through before serving.
- Serve with a little shaving of Parmesan.

Top tip: Swap the chicken for prawns for a delicious fishy dishy.

Honey and garlic chicken noodles

Press to plate

25 minutes

This is one of our Lils' absolute favourite chicken dishes, served with oodles of noodles in a sweet sticky sauce.

INGREDIENTS
4 nests of dried noodles
1 ½ tbsp sesame oil
2 tbsp light soy sauce
2 tbsp oyster sauce
2 tbsp honey
1 tbsp sweet chilli sauce
Pinch of Chinese 5 spice
4 free-range chicken
  breasts, sliced
3 tsp finely chopped
  ginger
2 garlic cloves, crushed
1 red pepper, deseeded
  and chopped
115g packet baby corn,
  halved
150g tenderstem broccoli
Sesame seeds, to serve

METHOD
- Place the noodles in a heatproof bowl. Cover with boiling water and set aside for 10 minutes to soak. Drain and drizzle with a little sesame oil to prevent them from sticking.
- Combine the soy sauce, oyster sauce, honey and sweet chilli sauce in a bowl.
- Meanwhile, heat 1 tablespoon of sesame oil in a wok over high heat.
- Add the chicken and cook for 3 minutes. Turn and cook for a further 3 minutes or until golden-brown.
- Add another drizzle of the oil to the wok with the ginger and garlic.
- Stir-fry for 3 minutes until aromatic. Add the red pepper, baby corn and tenderstem broccoli.
- Fry for another minute and cook until the vegetables are tender.
- Drizzle over your sauce and add the drained noodles to the wok. Use tongs to toss to combine.
- Sprinkle with sesame seeds to serve.

Top tip: It's important when cooking the marinated chicken to do it in batches and not to overcrowd the pan; that way the spices seal the chicken, adding a great depth of flavour.

Chicken tikka masala

Recreate this classic Indian dish at home – perfect for family gatherings as you can leave it simmering away until you're ready to serve.

Press to plate

50 minutes

INGREDIENTS

4 chicken breasts, sliced
For the chicken marinade
200g Greek yoghurt
   mixed with:
   1 minced garlic clove
   1 tsp minced ginger
   2 tsp garam masala
   1 tsp turmeric
   1 tsp mixed spice
   1 tsp ground cumin
   Pinch chilli powder
   Salt and pepper
For the sauce
2 tbsp rapeseed oil
2 tbsp salt-free butter
1 onion, finely diced
2 cloves of garlic, crushed
1 thumb-sized piece of
   ginger, minced
1 tbsp tomato puree
Pinch of sugar
1 tbsp curry powder
1 tsp garam masala
1 tsp ground cumin
1 tsp turmeric powder
1 tsp mixed spice
200g passata
100mls fresh cream
100mls water if needed
Coriander to garnish
   (optional)

METHOD

- In a bowl, combine chicken with all of the ingredients for the chicken marinade; let marinate for 10 minutes to an hour (or overnight if time allows).
- Heat 1 tablespoon of oil in a large pan over medium-high heat.
- Add chicken pieces to the pan in batches to sizzle, making sure not to overcrowd the pan.
- Fry until browned for 5 minutes. Set aside and keep warm. (You will finish cooking the chicken in the sauce.)
- Add 1 tbsp rapeseed oil and butter to melt to a saucepan.
- Sauté the onions until soft. Add garlic and ginger and fry for 1 minute until fragrant, then squeeze in tomato puree and add a pinch of sugar.
- Now add the spice to the pot: curry powder, garam masala, cumin, turmeric and mixed spice.
- Add the chicken back in the pot and stir to absorb all those gorgeous favours, add the passata and let simmer for about 10–15 minutes, stirring occasionally until sauce thickens and becomes a deep brown–red colour.
- Pour over the cream and cook for an additional 8–10 minutes until chicken is cooked through and the sauce is thick and bubbling.
- Add a little water if desired if sauce is too thick.

Sage and onion breaded chicken with savoury chicken gravy

Press to plate

55 minutes

This dish has all the flavour of a Sunday roast only it's cooked in half the time. Serve it with chips for a simple, midweek family meal.

INGREDIENTS

4 chicken breasts
250g plain flour mixed with:
  1 tsp paprika
  1 tsp smoked paprika
  1 tsp black pepper
  Pinch of cayenne pepper
4 free-range eggs

200g panko breadcrumbs mixed with:
  1 tbsp sage
  1 tbsp onion powder
  1 tbsp garlic powder
  Salt and pepper

For the gravy
1 tbsp salt-free butter

1 tbsp flour
1 tsp sage
400mls of chicken stock made with a stockpot
1 tsp Dijon mustard
Season with salt and a good shake of freshly ground black pepper

METHOD

- Preheat the oven to 180°C fan.
- Line an ovenproof dish with greaseproof paper.
- Prepare 3 medium-sized bowls: one with the seasoned flour, one with beaten egg, and one with the breadcrumbs and sage mix.
- Trim and flatten each chicken breast, removing any skin and fat and giving a little bash with a rolling pin to flatten.
- One at a time, cover each breast in flour then dredge in egg and completely cover in breadcrumbs. You can do the egg and crumb twice for extra coverage.
- Place chicken on your ovenproof dish and bake on the middle shelf for 45 minutes until chicken is cooked through.
- Meanwhile, make the gravy:
- In a saucepan melt the butter in the saucepan.
- Add flour and whisk into a smooth roux.
- Pour over the chicken stock, adding it 200mls at a time, whisking and letting it thicken each time.
- Add the mustard and finish with a good seasoning of freshly ground black pepper and a pinch of salt.
- Serve with chips and peas for a simple midweek roast.

Top tip: Slice your cooked, breaded chicken and serve in baguettes with mayo for a chicken-and-stuffing taste experience without the hassle of a roast.

Top tip: Up the veggie game with this one by adding matchstick carrots and peppers, baby corn and sliced spring onion.

Pineapple chicken

This dish has quickly become another huge family favourite. The sweetness from the pineapple makes it really popular with kids and adults alike.

Press to plate

25 minutes

INGREDIENTS

1 tbsp rapeseed oil
4 chicken breasts, diced
100g diced tinned pineapple
200mls pineapple juice (or just use the syrup from the tin)
2 tbsp soy sauce
2 tbsp oyster sauce
1 tbsp brown sugar
1 tbsp minced fresh garlic
120mls chicken stock
2 tsp cornflour mixed with a dribble of water
50g roasted cashews (optional)
Egg-fried rice for serving

METHOD

- Add the rapeseed oil to a wok over a medium heat.
- Add the chicken to the pan, season it with salt and pepper and cook for about 5 minutes.
- Add the pineapple and pineapple juice with the garlic, soy sauce, hoisin sauce and brown sugar.
- Bring to the boil for 5 minutes to evaporate the sugar.
- Pour over the chicken stock and simmer for another 5 minutes.
- Thicken with your cornflour paste.
- Finish with the roasted cashews, stirring for an additional 1 minute.
- Serve the chicken on a bed of egg-fried rice.

Top tip: If you're not a fan of chicken on the bone you can use chicken breasts, cooking them for 20 to 30 minutes.

Cajun chicken thighs

This is one of our favourite ways to eat chicken. Add corn on the cob and baby potatoes to the tray for 25 minutes cooking time to make a delicious all-in-one tray bake.

Press to plate

60 minutes

INGREDIENTS

6 chicken thighs

Spiced oil
3 tbsp rapeseed oil
1 tbsp oregano
1 tbsp Cajun spice
1 tsp paprika
1 tsp smoked paprika

METHOD

- Preheat oven to 180°C fan.
- Trim the skin of your chicken thighs and cut two slits in them (you can completely remove the skin to cut down on the fat content).
- Arrange the chicken thighs on a large baking sheet.
- Mix your oil with the spices and brush onto the skin or the top of each chicken thigh.
- Bake for 50 minutes until the skin is crispy and the chicken is cooked through.

Jolene and Lily Mae cooking together.

This has to be one of my very favorite photos of myself and Lils cooking together at home. The moment was captured by Simon Walsh while he was shooting a video for our Family Cooking Club. Lils is aged 6 in this photo and is quite happily making our hidden veggie marinara sauce (from page 37), with a little assistance from myself.

Chapter Two

Just Veg

Falafel pittas

These simple falafels are so easy to put together for a midweek veggie treat. Serve them simply with hummus and couscous or fill them into toasted pittas with fresh salad leaves. This recipe makes 12 falafels.

Press to plate

30 minutes

INGREDIENTS

1 can chickpeas (drained, rinsed and patted dry)
1 red pepper
A bunch chopped fresh parsley
2 cloves garlic, minced

2 scallions, sliced
2 tbsp sesame seeds
1 tsp cumin
1 tsp mixed spice
1 tsp curry
Rind of ½ lemon

A good seasoning of salt and pepper
3–4 tbsp all-purpose flour (or ground almonds)
100g panko breadcrumbs or regular breadcrumbs for coating

METHOD

- Add chickpeas, parsley, scallion, garlic, sesame seeds, ground spices, salt and pepper to a food processor or blender and pulse to combine, making sure you leave some lumps in. You are not looking for a smooth paste!
- Remove from the mixer, add to a large bowl with the flour and grate in the lemon rind.
- Flour your hands, then get them in and roll the mixture into 12 balls.
- Roll each falafel in the breadcrumbs.
- Add to a lined baking sheet, drizzle with a little rapeseed oil and oven bake at 180°C fan for 20 minutes.
- Toast your pittas and fill with lettuce and cucumber; serve with a drizzle of chilli sauce and mayonnaise.

Top tip: Mould into 6 patties to make delicious veggie burgers and top with our homemade burger sauce from page 5.

Roasted veggie pasta bake

Press to plate

40 minutes

- We can never have enough pasta bake recipes up our sleeves and this one is always on the meal plan for a meat-free evening. Deliciously filling and packed with healthy veg.

INGREDIENTS

300g fusilli pasta
1 tbsp rapeseed oil
1 onion, diced
2 garlic cloves, crushed
3 beef tomatoes, deseeded and diced
1 red pepper, sliced

1 courgette, diced
½ butternut squash, diced
1 tbsp tomato puree
Pinch of sugar
1 tbsp oregano, dried
200g mixed mozzarella and cheddar

METHOD

- Preheat the oven to 220°C fan.
- On a flat baking sheet, toss the pepper, courgette, squash, onions and garlic with oil.
- Sprinkle with oregano and season with salt and pepper. Roast until tender, about 10 minutes.
- Meanwhile cook pasta al dente for around 6 minutes.
- Mix the drained pasta with the roasted vegetables in a large bowl. Add tomato puree and a pinch of sugar to offset the acidity of the tomato puree.
- Pour the pasta and veggies into an ovenproof dish.
- Sprinkle with cheese and bake the whole lot together at 180°C fan for about 30 minutes, until top is golden and cheese melts.

Top tip: If you like your pasta bake nice and creamy, add 200g of mascarpone cheese.

Mozzarella, spinach and roasted red pepper tart

Press to plate

30 minutes

This dish has some serious summer vibes – perfect for dining al fresco or for a fancy picnic treat. One of those throw-together recipes that taste divine.

INGREDIENTS

- 1 pack of shortcrust pastry
- 1 tbsp tomato relish
- 1 quality ball of mozzarella
- 200g cherry tomatoes, halved
- 1 red pepper, sliced
- 100g green olives, sliced
- 5 torn basil leaves
- A handful of fresh rocket

METHOD

- Preheat oven to 180°C fan.
- Roll out your shortcrust pastry onto a baking tray lined with greaseproof paper.
- Spread with the relish and add torn mozzarella.
- Half the tomatoes and slice the red pepper, and scatter evenly over the pastry.
- Finish with the olives and torn basil leaves.
- Oven bake for 30 minutes.
- Add the rocket and place it back into the oven for 5 minutes.
- Slice into 6 pieces and devour.

Top tip: Swap the shortcrust pastry to puff pastry, roll and slice to make delicious pastry pinwheels.

Classic Greek salad

Apart from a huge Irish mammy salad with cold meats and homemade coleslaw, this has to be top of the list on a summer's day.

Press to plate

15 minutes

INGREDIENTS

200g cherry tomatoes, halved
½ cucumber, diced
½ red onion, thinly sliced
50g green olives
50g black olives
150g feta cheese, cut into cubes
1 tsp dried oregano
2 tbsp extra virgin olive oil
2 tbsp balsamic vinegar

METHOD

- Place sliced tomatoes, cucumber, red onions and feta into a large bowl.
- Season and add the olives.
- Sprinkle over dried oregano, lightly season with salt and pepper.
- Mix together the oil and balsamic vinegar and drizzle on top.
- Serve with crusty bread to mop up all of those delicious juices.

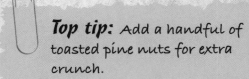

Top tip: Add a handful of toasted pine nuts for extra crunch.

Broccoli three-cheese filo

I absolutely love the crunch when cutting into filo pastry. The three cheeses work so well in this tart and there's no waste as you even use the broccoli stalk!

Press to plate

45 minutes

INGREDIENTS

1 large head of broccoli
100g cheddar, grated
200g mascarpone
100g cream cheese

1 tsp nutmeg
1 tsp Dijon mustard
4 sheets of filo pastry
150g butter, melted

METHOD

- Preheat oven to 150°C fan.
- Chop the broccoli, including the stalks, and boil until tender.
- When cooked, crumble the broccoli into a large bowl along with the cheeses, nutmeg and Dijon mustard, and mix. Add salt and pepper.
- Lay one sheet of filo pastry onto a large baking sheet and brush with melted butter.
- Add another sheet on top and brush with butter again.
- Pile the broccoli mix onto the pastry sheets and spread out to a rectangle.
- Top with one sheet of filo and brush with butter and add another sheet on top.
- Tuck the pastry in at the sides and brush with butter on the top.
- Place into the middle of the oven and bake for 30 minutes.

Top tip: You can swap the broccoli for cauliflower or even do half and half to change things up.

31

Rainbow veggie rolls

These little rainbow rolls are great fun to make. If you stir-fry the veggies and place them in a bowl the kids will really enjoy making them into little spring rolls.

Press to plate

30 minutes

INGREDIENTS

3 spring onions
1 red pepper
1 red onion
1 green pepper
1 carrot
2 cm piece of ginger
2 garlic cloves
2 tbsp soy sauce
2 tbsp oyster sauce
1 tbsp sweet chilli sauce
1 tsp Chinese 5 spice
8 sheets of filo pastry
1 tbsp melted butter

METHOD

- Slice your veggies into matchstick slices, peel and crush garlic and grate ginger.
- Place a wok over a medium heat with good drizzle of sesame oil and fry veggies until softened.
- Add the soy, oyster, and sweet chilli sauces, along with the Chinese 5 spice.
- One at a time, brush each sheet with butter and add the filling to the centre. Roll each one, tucking in the corners, and brush with butter or sesame oil.
- Place onto a lined baking tray.
- Oven bake at 180°C fan on the middle shelf for 15 to 20 minutes until they are golden and crispy.

Top tip: You can get the kids to pick and choose what veggies they would like to add. If that involves just adding stir-fried carrots, so be it, we can call them carrot rolls!

33

Top tip: Slice into goujon shapes and cook the same way to make some delicious cheesy dippers!

Halloumi burger with sweet chilli sauce

Press to plate

25 minutes

Having only discovered the joy of halloumi last year, I just love its versatility. It tastes great in salads and curries, but I have to say the halloumi burger really tops it in the taste department. This recipe makes four burgers.

INGREDIENTS

3 tbsp rapeseed oil
500g/2 blocks halloumi
100g cornflour
1 tbsp garlic powder
1 tbsp onion powder
1 tsp smoked paprika
A good shake of black
  pepper and salt

To serve
4 brioche buns
Sweet chilli sauce
A handful of rocket for
  each bun

METHOD

- Heat the oil in a frying pan over a medium heat.
- Cut each halloumi block in half along the centre so you end up with a square burger shape.
- Mix the cornflour, paprika, and seasonings on a plate.
- Brush each halloumi piece with oil and coat both sides with the cornflour and spice mix.
- Oil a non-stick pan and fry for 5 minutes on each side.
- Try not to move them around the pan so much so they don't loose their crispy coating.
- Serve on dressed buns with sweet chilli sauce.

Top tip: This makes a delicious ragu sauce if you are brave enough to leave it chunky.

Hidden veggie marinara sauce

Press to plate
50 minutes

As you may know, I'm always trying to come up with clever ways to sneak nutrients into Lils, and this recipe ticks all the boxes. It's packed to the brim with veggie goodness, and the crowning glory is if you have any fussy eaters, they won't be able to tell there are any vegetables in there at all!

INGREDIENTS

2 red onions
2 celery stalks
3 garlic cloves
2 red peppers
1 carrot
3 beef tomatoes
½ butternut squash
1 small leek
1 tbsp balsamic vinegar
200g passata
400mls chicken or
   vegetable stock
1 tbsp dried oregano
1 tsp brown sugar
20g Parmesan (optional)

METHOD

- Prepare your veggies: peel and dice the red onions, carrot and squash; peel and crush your garlic cloves; slice the celery, leek, red pepper and beef tomatoes.
- Place a heavy-based saucepan over a medium heat with a glug of olive oil.
- Start by sautéing the red onion and crushed garlic for 5 minutes until soft and the onion has slightly caramelised.
- Pour in a tablespoon of balsamic vinegar and let it infuse for a minute.
- Add in the rest of the prepared vegetables and mix well.
- Sprinkle in the oregano and season with a little salt and pepper.
- Give a good mix before pouring in the passata and stock.
- Cover with a lid and turn the heat down low, leaving the sauce to simmer for 40 minutes.
- After 40 minutes, check the squash with a knife to ensure that it's soft and completely cooked through.
- Add in a teaspoon of brown sugar and blend the sauce until smooth.
- Finish by adding 20g grated Parmesan; this is optional but adds a great depth of flavour.

Cream cheese and cherry tomato fusilli

Press to plate

30 minutes

There were a few variations of this cream cheese pasta bake online earlier this year, but this is my take on it.

INGREDIENTS

400g fusilli
200g full-fat cream
   cheese
1 tbsp oregano
A good drizzle of olive oil
150g cherry tomatoes
2 garlic cloves
1 red pepper
Handful of fresh basil
   leaves to garnish

METHOD

- Cook fusilli according to the packet instructions.
- Meanwhile preheat oven to 180°C fan.
- In an ovenproof dish scatter tomatoes, diced red pepper, and crushed garlic.
- Add a good drizzle of olive oil.
- Place your cream cheese in the middle of the dish.
- Oven bake for 30 minutes.
- Drain your pasta and add it to the dish.
- Give a good mix and finish with a scattering of fresh basil.

Top tip: Other vegetables that work well are diced courgette and butternut squash.

Red pepper and butternut squash soup

Press to plate

30 minutes

This is one of our favourite family soups at the minute, served steaming hot, bowl filled to the brim and with a side of delicious garlic bread.

INGREDIENTS

1 white onion
2 garlic cloves
½ butternut squash
1 carrot
2 red peppers
1 x 400g tin chopped
   tomatoes
200mls vegetable stock
½ can coconut milk (using
   the creamed coconut
   on top)

METHOD

- In a large saucepan with a lid place roughly chopped onion and garlic and add a tablespoon of rapeseed oil; cook for 5 minutes to soften.
- Add diced butternut squash, red pepper and carrot.
- Pour over the tinned tomatoes, stock and coconut milk.
- Simmer for 30 minutes with a lid on.
- Blend and serve.

Top tip: If you are not a fan of coconut milk just add cream instead.

During lockdown myself and Lils decided to run weekly kids in the kitchen cook-alongs. Each week there were over 50 households joining us in our kitchen for an online cook-along every Wednesday at 1 p.m. It was the perfect time for the kids to cook lunch and the family to eat it together. The sessions are led by Lily Mae, meaning she does the actual cooking and I just facilitate and guide. The feedback from this format has been so positive as the kids relate so well to another kid. They are very light-hearted and great fun, and the children get a well-earned break from homeschooling. This is a style of cook-along we have continued each week in our Family Cooking Club.

Chapter Three

Meat Up Again

Top tip: If you have a party, this recipe will also cover up to 16 mini-sliders using mini burger buns.

American double bacon cheeseburgers

Press to plate

30 minutes

I remember having a double bacon cheeseburger for dinner in Las Vegas 11 years ago and it has stayed with me since. The thin strips of American-style bacon are now readily available in Irish supermarkets, so I couldn't wait to recreate this classic at home. This recipe makes four servings.

INGREDIENTS

800g mince beef (10% fat will give good flavour)
12 slices of American-style bacon
2 tbsp Worcestershire sauce
A good seasoning of salt and black pepper
4 slices of cheddar cheese
4 gherkins
4 brioche buns
Sliced iceberg lettuce

For burger sauce
2 tbsp American mustard
4 tbsp mayonnaise

METHOD

- Preheat oven to 180°C fan.
- In a large mixing bowl add the mince, season with salt and pepper and add Worcestershire sauce.
- Get your hands in and give a good mix.
- Divide into 8 balls and flatten each ball down into patties.
- Add the burgers to an oven sheet lined with greaseproof paper and oven cook for 20 minutes (by cooking the burgers this way they turn out really juicy and don't break up).
- Meanwhile over a medium heat add a drizzle of oil to a medium frying pan.
- Fry the bacon until crispy and chewy.
- After 20 minutes top the burgers with cheese and place back into the oven on the middle shelf.
- Brush the brioche buns with a little melted butter and toast in the oven on the bottom shelf for 5 minutes.
- Make the burger sauce by mixing the mayo and mustard together.
- Dress your buns with lettuce at the bottom and fried bacon and burger sauce on top and stack two burgers each inside.
- Serve with a simple salad and chips.

Top tip: These also taste great using turkey mince or changing up the flavour with a chicken stock cube.

Swedish meatballs

There's no need to get your Swedish meatball fix while buying flat pack furniture anymore! You can now make this simple classic at home.

Press to plate

40 minutes

INGREDIENTS

For the meatballs

800g lean beef mince

2 crushed garlic cloves

1 tsp Worcestershire sauce

1 tsp garlic powder

1 tsp onion powder

1 grated or blended onion (it's very important you grate the onion as it gives the meatballs a little moisture)

A bunch of fresh parsley and thyme, chopped

For the sauce

1 onion, finely chopped

2 crushed garlic cloves

100g mushrooms, sliced

1 heaped tsp Dijon mustard

1 beef stock cube or stock pot in 300mls of water

1 tsp cranberry sauce

2 heaped tbsp crème fraîche

METHOD

- Preheat oven to 180°C fan.
- Grate onion and crush your garlic.
- Chop the fresh herbs finely and add all the meatball ingredients to a mixing bowl.
- Get your hands in and give a good mix.
- Mould 12 meatballs and add them to a mini muffin tin; oven bake for 20 minutes.

For the sauce

- Put your saucepan over medium heat with a little oil.
- Soften the chopped onion and garlic for your sauce.
- Put in your sliced mushroom and cook for 5 minutes.
- Add Dijon mustard and season with salt and pepper.
- Pour over the beef stock, add the cranberry sauce and let simmer for 10 minutes as the meatballs finish off in the oven.
- When the meatballs are cooked add them to the pot and finish with a good dollop of crème fraiche.
- Serve with fluffy rice.

Honey and mustard sizzling chops

Press to plate

45 minutes

Honey and mustard are a perfect flavour combo for pork chops. By oven-baking the chops they won't dry out like they can on the pan. This is another perfect midweeker, served simply with peas and creamy mash.

INGREDIENTS

4 thick boneless pork chops
4 tbsp Dijon mustard
4 tbsp runny honey
1 tsp ground black pepper
A good pinch of salt and pepper

METHOD

- Preheat oven to 180°C fan and line a baking dish.
- Mix Dijon mustard, honey, black pepper, and salt together in a bowl.
- Arrange pork chops in a prepared baking dish and brush half the mustard mixture over pork.
- Oven bake for 20 minutes, turn the chops and brush again with the rest of the mustard and honey mix.
- Cook for another 20 minutes.
- Crisp up the fat by finishing under the grill for 5 minutes.

Top tip: Don't forget to crisp up the fat under the grill for that extra sizzle!

Sausage and egg muffin

Homemade sausage and egg muffins taste better than any fast-food takeout. An added bonus: you can make them at any time of the day so they're not just for breakfast.

Press to plate

25 minutes

INGREDIENTS

200g sausage meat (remove skins from your favourite brand of sausages)
1 tbsp sage
1 tbsp flour
4 eggs
4 English muffins

METHOD

- Mix the sausage meat, flour and dried sage together in a large bowl.
- Flour your hands and shape the sausage meat mix into thin burgers, approximately two centimetres thick.
- Fry in a pan drizzled with rapeseed oil until crisp on both sides; it usually only takes 5 minutes each side.
- Toast your muffins.
- Fry the eggs to your liking.
- Then assemble the muffins with the patties, add the egg and serve immediately.

Top tip: Melt on some smoked cheese slices to up the flavour game.

Taco fries and epic garlic mayo

Press to plate

55 minutes

When running my schools parents' programme, I always ask if there is a takeaway dish they would like to make homemade and healthier. This taco fries recipe was a total winner. Once you make the garlic mayo like this there is no turning back to shop-bought.

INGREDIENTS

For the mince
500g lean mince
1 onion, diced
2 garlic cloves, crushed
1 red pepper, sliced
1 green pepper, sliced

Taco seasoning
1 tbsp smoked paprika
1 tbsp cumin
¼ tsp cayenne pepper
1 tsp oregano
½ tsp salt

½ tsp black pepper

Garlic mayo
2 tbsp good-quality mayonnaise
2 garlic cloves, crushed
1 tsp salt

Homemade chips
4 new potatoes

Handful of grated cheddar cheese

METHOD

- Preheat oven to 180°C fan.
- In a large pan over medium heat fry onion and garlic in a glug of rapeseed oil.
- When softened add mince, breaking it up as you fry it.
- When the mince is browned drain off any fat in the pan.
- Add in red and green pepper and homemade Taco seasoning and simmer for 40 minutes.
- Meanwhile make your chips by peeling and chipping your potatoes.
- Parboil in hot seasoned water for 6 minutes.
- Arrange chips on an ovenproof sheet and drizzle with rapeseed oil.
- Cook in a preheated oven for 50 minutes, giving them a shake after 25 minutes.
- Serve the chips with a generous portion of taco mince, followed by a tablespoon of garlic mayo and finish with a scattering of cheddar over the top.

Top tip: This is also delicious on baked potatoes. Want that baked potato taste in half the time? Wash and pierce 2 medium-sized new potatoes and microwave for 5 minutes. When softened in the middle, drizzle with rapeseed oil and oven bake at 200°C fan for 20 minutes.

Beef stroganoff

This is a wholesome, midweek family favourite of ours.
Serve it with rice, on baked potatoes or with creamy mash.
And it's even more delicious on a cold, blustery evening.

Press to plate

4 hours

INGREDIENTS

500g stewing beef pieces
1 red onion, diced
2 garlic cloves, crushed
½ pack of button
  mushrooms, sliced
1 tbsp plain flour
1 heaped tsp smoked
  paprika
1 heaped tsp sweet
  paprika
1 tbsp American mustard
  (it was the only one
  I had, any mustard
  would do except for
  whole grain)
1 beef stock cube in
  400mls warm water
Dollop of crème fraîche
  or sour cream

METHOD

- Brown beef in a large deep casserole pot with a lid, in a little oil. Remove from the pot after 5 minutes.
- Soften onion and garlic, add mushrooms and then put the beef back in.
- Season with a little salt and pepper
- Add the flour; this will soak up any delicious juices and thicken your sauce.
- Add paprika and mustard and mix.
- Slowly pour in beef stock, stirring as you add it.
- Cover with a lid and simmer for 3.5 hours,
- Add a good dollop of crème fraîche or sour cream after 3.5 hours.
- Garnish with fresh parsley and serve with rice.

Top tip: This is another dish that makes a tasty pie filling, just top with a ready-made puff pastry lid and bake in the oven for 40 minutes at 180°C fan.

Top tip: Add some king prawns for a delicious surf and turf in minutes.

Steak strip wok noodles

We all have those evenings where we want a delish meal we can cook in 15 minutes that the whole family will eat! This is the one.

Press to plate

15 minutes

INGREDIENTS

1 tbsp sesame oil
1 onion, sliced
1 green pepper, sliced
2 sirloin steaks, sliced into strips
1 tbsp oyster sauce
1 tsp rice wine vinegar
1 tsp sweet chilli sauce
1 tbsp brown sugar
A good squeeze of lime juice

METHOD

- Add sesame oil to a wok and place on a high heat. Stir-fry onion and green pepper for 5 minutes until the onion is golden and caramelised.
- To the wok add your sliced sirloin steaks and stir-fry for another 5 minutes.
- Dollop in a tablespoon each of oyster sauce and brown sugar, and a teaspoon each of rice wine vinegar and sweet chilli sauce.
- Finish with a squeeze of lime juice.
- Serve with simple boiled noodles.

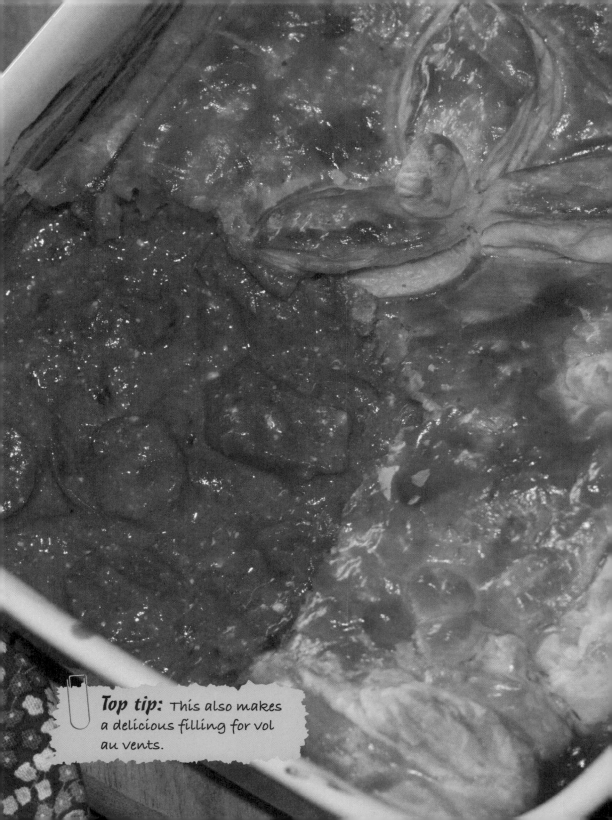

Top tip: This also makes a delicious filling for vol au vents.

Beef goulash and chorizo pie

Beef goulash is a huge family classic in our house, but by adding chorizo and topping with a puff pastry hat we are really upping the midweek meal game.

Press to plate

4 hours
40 minutes

(but well worth the wait)

INGREDIENTS

1 tsp olive oil/ a few sprays of Frylight
450g stewing beef pieces (remove all visible fat)
1 tbsp plain flour
1 large onion, chopped
2 cloves of garlic, minced
3 large tomatoes, diced
1 red pepper, thinly sliced
2 tbsp tomato puree
1 tbsp sweet paprika
½ tbsp smoked paprika
300ml beef stock
1 tbsp crème fraîche
100g chorizo
1 pack of puff pastry

METHOD

- Heat a teaspoon of olive oil in a casserole dish or heavy-based saucepan. Sprinkle the beef with the flour and brown well on a medium heat.
- Add onion, garlic, tomatoes and red pepper to the pan with the beef. Fry until softened, add the tomato puree and both types of paprika and give a good mix.
- Finally, pour over the beef stock, cover and cook it on the hob on a gentle heat for about 4 hours.
- Dollop in the crème fraîche and give a good stir, making sure the crème fraîche is well mixed in.
- Transfer to an ovenproof pie dish and add sliced chorizo.
- Top with puff pastry and brush with egg.
- Oven bake at 180°C fan for 40 minutes.
- Serve with creamy mash.

Top tip: This recipe also makes a perfect lasagne, just swap the aubergine for pasta sheets and cook the very same way.

Moussaka with cheat's béchamel sauce

Press to plate

1 hour

Moussaka is the perfect use for those aubergines you never know what to do with. Teamed with a cheat's white sauce (so no standing around stirring the pot), this makes a delicious, tasty meal for something a little different.

INGREDIENTS

1 aubergine
1 tsp salt
3 tbsp rapeseed oil
1 onion, sliced
3 garlic cloves, crushed
800g minced beef
1 x 400g tin chopped
   tomatoes
3 tbsp tomato paste
1 bay leaf
Pinch of sugar
1 tbsp dried oregano

Cheat's béchamel sauce
200g mascarpone cheese
200mls chicken stock
1 tsp Dijon mustard
1 tsp nutmeg

200g Mozzarella and
   Cheddar cheese, grated

METHOD

- Start by slicing the aubergine, patting it dry, drizzle with oil and bake at 160°C fan for 20 minutes until softened.
- Remove and set aside to cool slightly.
- Meanwhile make your filling. Heat a drizzle of oil in oil over high heat and cook the garlic and onion for 2 minutes.
- Add the mince and cook until it changes from pink to brown, breaking it up as you go.
- Add remaining ingredients and stir to combine and cook for a further 15 minutes.
- Leave to simmer while you make your cheat's béchamel sauce. Over a gentle heat in a small saucepan add mascarpone cheese, chicken stock, Dijon mustard and nutmeg, and stir until you have a delicious, smooth white sauce.
- Preheat the oven to 180°C fan.
- Place half the aubergine in the bottom of a baking dish then layer up like a lasagne: add mince, pour over the béchamel sauce, then sprinkle with a mix of mozzarella and cheddar. I like to make three layers.
- Bake for 30–40 minutes or until golden brown. Allow to stand for 10 minutes before serving.

Enchiladas

I think we all have that one pack of mince hanging around at the back of the freezer. These tasty enchiladas are the perfect way to bring it to life.

Press to plate

40 minutes

INGREDIENTS

1 tbsp rapeseed oil, plus extra for greasing
500g beef mince
1 red pepper
1 onion, finely diced
3 garlic cloves, crushed
1 x 400g tin chopped tomatoes
1 tbsp tomato paste

1 tbsp cumin
1 tbsp oregano
1 tsp smoked paprika
Pinch of chilli powder
Salt and freshly ground black pepper
8 soft tortilla wraps (regular size)
200g cheddar, grated
Crème fraîche, to serve (optional)

METHOD

- Heat a large pan with a drizzle of rapeseed oil on a medium heat. Add the onion and garlic, cooking for 4 minutes until softened
- Add the mince to the pan, breaking up with a wooden spoon, and brown well.
- Sprinkle over the herbs and spices, stirring for 4 minutes to help release the flavour.
- Pour over tomatoes and bring to the boil, then reduce the heat to simmer for 5 minutes, until thickened.
- Preheat the oven to 180°C fan.
- Lightly oil a shallow ovenproof dish.
- Fill each tortilla with a good spoonful of the mixture, roll and line up in your prepared dish.
- Scatter with grated cheddar. Bake for 20 minutes, serve with a dollop of crème fraîche.

Top tip: This is also a great way to give your leftover spag bol a new lease of life.

This was taken at the Dualla Show back in 2019.

The Dualla Show is a family fun festival in the heart of Tipperary. I absolutely love live cooking demos and this one was pretty special as it was live in the marquee, giving off huge *Bake-Off* vibes. I cooked a selection of dishes the whole family could enjoy. The tent was absolutely packed on the day and the atmosphere was just electric. It took me a few days to calm down, one to remember.

Chapter Four

Curry Night

Top tip: This is also a great slow-cooker curry. Just throw all the ingredients into the slow cooker for 3½ hours on high or 7 hours on low.

Scratch chicken curry

This is hotly becoming one of the most popular curries since my chicken curry in a hurry from my first book. It's so easy to put together and by making your own curry paste, you know exactly what's gone into it.

Press to plate

50 minutes

INGREDIENTS

4 free-range chicken
   breasts, sliced

Homemade curry paste

2 tbsp tomato puree

1 tbsp mango chutney

2 tbsp curry powder (mild
   or medium)

1 tsp turmeric

1 tsp cumin

1 tsp ground mixed spice

1 tsp ground coriander

400ml coconut milk

200ml chicken stock

METHOD

- In a small mixing bowl make up your home-made curry paste: Mix together 2 tablespoons of tomato puree, 1 tablespoon of mango chutney, 2 tablespoons of curry powder and 1 teaspoon each of turmeric, mixed spice, ground coriander and cumin.
- Place the saucepan over a medium heat with a glug of rapeseed oil. Add the sliced chicken breasts and cook for 5 minutes, stirring frequently to ensure they don't stick.
- Now spoon your homemade curry paste over the chicken breasts. Sizzle for 5 minutes, the aroma will be absolutely amazing!
- Pour over the coconut milk and hot chicken stock. Cover with a lid and simmer over a low heat for 20 minutes.
- Serve with boiled rice, your favourite mixed veg and a garnish of fresh coriander.

Top tip: Fancy upping the veggie intake even more? Add 200g of cauliflower florets and 1 diced butternut squash and cook for an extra 10 minutes.

Thai veggie curry

Fresh, crunchy and eating all the colours of the rainbow is the only way to describe this curry; such a delicious way to get in your five a day.

Press to plate

25 minutes

INGREDIENTS

1 onion, sliced
1 red pepper, sliced
1 green pepper, sliced
100g baby corn
100g tenderstem broccoli
1 carrot, chopped into matchsticks
1 tbsp tomato puree
300ml hot chicken stock
1 x 400g can full-fat coconut milk

For the curry paste

1 tbsp rapeseed or melted coconut oil
1 tbsp mild curry powder
1 tsp cumin
1 tsp coriander
1 tsp dried red chilli flakes
4 crushed garlic cloves
1 centimetre cubed piece of fresh ginger, grated
1 tsp lemongrass puree
½ lime, zested
1 tsp fish sauce

METHOD

- Prepare your curry paste by mashing garlic, ginger, lime zest, spices and oil together in a pestle and mortar or a bowl until you have a paste.
- Heat a drizzle of rapeseed oil over a medium heat. Fry your onion and pepper in the saucepan for around 3 minutes.
- Add baby corn, tenderstem broccoli and matchstick carrots.
- Squeeze in the tomato puree and season with salt and pepper. Add your homemade curry paste to the pot.
- Pour in the chicken stock and make sure all the vegetables are immersed in the liquid. Cover and simmer for 15 minutes.
- Add your coconut milk and simmer for another minute.
- Serve with a squeeze of fresh lime juice and some extra chillies and coriander for the experimental family members!
- This dish is perfect teamed with simple basmati rice.

Salmon curry parcels

Another easy way to get fish into the family, this parcel steaming technique works really well with chicken too. This recipe makes one salmon parcel per person.

Press to plate

40 minutes

INGREDIENTS

1 sheet of greaseproof paper per person
1 salmon darne per person
1 tbsp tomato puree
1 tbsp rapeseed oil
1 tbsp curry powder
1 tsp ground ginger
1 tsp turmeric

METHOD

- Preheat oven to 180°C fan.
- Fold your sheet of greaseproof paper in half. Open the paper out and add your salmon to one side of the paper.
- Meanwhile make your curry paste by mixing the tomato puree with the spices. Spread each salmon darne with the curry paste.
- Add a drizzle of rapeseed oil. Fold over the top of the greaseproof paper and seal the edges by twisting the paper. You will end up with a semi-circle parcel.
- Oven bake for 15–20 minutes.

Top tip: You can also add vegetables to each parcel, such as scallions, tenderstem broccoli or sliced red pepper.

Curried baked cauliflower

Press to plate

45 minutes

Once you try baking cauliflower there is no turning back, it will become the only way you cook it. Once baked it takes on a delicious nutty flavour, and teamed with the curry power it's a match made in heaven.

INGREDIENTS

2 tbsp rapeseed oil
1 tbsp curry powder
1 head of cauliflower

METHOD

- Preheat oven to 180°C fan.
- Chop the cauliflower florets and stalks.
- Place in a large bowl and completely cover in the curry powder and oil.
- Add to an ovenproof tray and bake for 40 minutes.

Top tip: You can mix it up by adding broccoli and diced butternut squash for a veggie curry tray bake.

Top tip: You can replace the apricot jam with honey if you prefer, but the jam does give a great depth of flavour.

Fragrant beef curry

Out of all my curries, this fragrant beef curry is my personal favourite. The jam gives it a delicious sweetness and the cream makes it so smooth. This is another curry dish that's great to have up your sleeve for a family gathering.

Press to plate

4 hours

INGREDIENTS

A drizzle of rapeseed oil
800g lean beef pieces
1 large white onion
2 large garlic cloves
1 thumb-sized piece of
   fresh ginger
½ red chilli (optional)
1 red pepper
140g tomato paste (small
   tin)
1 heaped tbsp apricot jam
   (trust me)
3 tbsp mild/medium
   curry powder
1 tsp turmeric
1 tsp brown sugar
500ml beef stock
100ml cream

METHOD

- Start by finely dicing your onion, crushing the garlic, and grating the ginger. Chop the chilli into tiny dice.
- In a large heavy-based saucepan with a lid heat a drizzle of rapeseed oil. Add onion, ginger, garlic and chillies into the saucepan and cook until softened.
- Add the beef, browning it all over.
- Mix together the tomato paste, apricot jam, brown sugar, curry powder and turmeric to make your curry paste. Add to the pot and give a good mix.
- Add diced red pepper and beef stock. Bring to the boil and then to a low simmer.
- Cover with a lid and simmer gently for 3.5 hours, checking the liquid a few times and topping up with water if needed.
- Finish with cream and a scattering of fresh coriander leaves.

Top tip: Cut the fat content in half by replacing the coconut milk with coconut yogurt.

Chicken koftas in korma sauce

Press to plate

45 minutes

This is a huge hit with the smallies! The korma is so mild it's a great introduction to curry for very young kids. And as an added bonus, they will just love to help by moulding and rolling the koftas. This recipe makes 9 koftas.

INGREDIENTS

For the koftas
400g chicken or turkey mince
100g breadcrumbs
2 garlic cloves
1 onion, diced
1 cubed centimetre ginger, grated
1 tbsp mild curry powder
Salt and freshly ground black pepper, to taste
Small handful of chopped fresh parsley

For the korma sauce
1 onion, diced
2 garlic cloves, crushed
1 centimetre cubed piece of ginger, grated
2 tbsp tomato puree
1 tbsp mild curry powder
1 tbsp garam masala
1 tsp sweet paprika
1 tsp turmeric
1 x 400g can coconut milk

METHOD

- First make the koftas. Preheat the oven to 180°C fan. Crush garlic and chop ginger and parsley.
- Add chicken mince to a large mixing bowl. Season with salt and pepper and add in the breadcrumbs, onion, garlic, and ginger.
- Sprinkle in the curry powder and get your hands in and give a good mix.
- Roll into 9 meatballs.
- Add to a flat baking tray and oven bake for 20 minutes.
- While the meatballs are cooking make your sauce: put a little coconut oil or rapeseed a large pan. Fry garlic and ginger.
- Add diced onion and soften.
- Add tomato puree and then the spices.
- Finish with coconut milk and simmer for 15 minutes.
- Add the cooked koftas and serve with rice.

71

Top tip: This curry can be blended to hide the veg for any veg-phobic smallies (shh, I won't tell them if you don't!).

Butternut squash and spinach curry

Press to plate

45 minutes

This is my go-to veggie option for family gatherings and it's a huge hit with meat-eaters and veggies alike so you can't go wrong with it.

INGREDIENTS

2 cloves of garlic, crushed
1 small red onion, diced
1 tbsp tomato puree
1 butternut squash, diced
½ green pepper, diced
100g mushrooms, sliced
A handful of spinach
300ml vegetable stock
200ml coconut milk
Salt and freshly ground
    black pepper, to taste

For the spice
2 tbsp curry powder
1 tsp each (ground)
    Cumin
    Coriander
    Garlic powder
    Onion powder
    Mixed spice
A pinch of chilli powder
    (optional)

METHOD

- Put your saucepan over a medium heat with a little oil and soften onion and garlic on the pan.
- Squeeze over the tomato puree and mix together. Sprinkle over curry powder and other spices.
- Add the diced butternut squash and green pepper, and season with a little salt and pepper.
- Add in your sliced mushroom, pour over the stock and coconut milk, stir and put on the lid and simmer for 25 minutes.
- Finally, add a handful of spinach and let it wilt.
- Scatter over a little chilli and fresh coriander to serve (optional).

Top tip: This sauce is also delicious slow-cooked with pork fillet. Just add the pork fillet to the slow cooker, pour over your sauce and cook for 4 hours on high or 7–8 on low.

Pork belly in peanut satay sauce

Press to plate

45 minutes

Pork and peanuts are a match made in heaven. Mixed with fragrant Asian spices, this is the ultimate way to eat pork belly.

INGREDIENTS

Drizzle of rapeseed oil
500g pork belly seasoned with salt and pepper

Peanut sauce
A drizzle of sesame oil or rapeseed oil
1 onion, diced
2 garlic cloves, crushed
1 centimetre cubed of fresh ginger, grated
2 tbsp mild curry powder (or hot if you like it spicy)
1 tbsp soy sauce
3 tbsp sweet chilli sauce
3 tbsp crunchy peanut butter
150ml water

METHOD

- Preheat oven to 180°C fan.
- Pat the pork belly dry with a little kitchen roll and add to a prepared ovenproof dish. Season with salt and pepper and drizzle with rapeseed oil.
- Oven bake for 40 minutes, turning after 20.
- Meanwhile, make your peanut sauce: put a small saucepan over a medium heat with a drizzle of sesame oil.
- Add diced onion, crushed garlic and grated ginger and cook for 3 minutes until softened.
- Add the curry powder and cook for a minute. Finish the sauce by adding crunchy peanut butter, sweet chilli sauce and soy sauce, stirring for 5 minutes until all the ingredients combine.
- Top up with 150mls of water.
- Check your pork belly and finish for a minute under the grill to crisp up the skin if needed.
- Pour the peanut sauce over the pork belly and serve with stir-fried veg and noodles.

Top tip: To mix the flavours up, you can use half sweet potato and half baby potato.

Bombay potatoes

This Indian side dish is so easy to put together and is the perfect accompaniment to any curry feast.

Press to plate

30 minutes

INGREDIENTS

400g baby potatoes
1 thumb-sized piece
　ginger, grated
2 large garlic cloves, crush
1 tbsp tomato paste
3 tbsp rapeseed oil
2 tsp ground coriander
1 tsp ground ginger
1 tsp turmeric
1 tsp ground cumin
1 tsp garam masala
Small bunch coriander,
　chopped

METHOD

- In a large mixing bowl grate the ginger, crush the garlic and mix together with the tomato paste, oil and spices.
- Put the potatoes in a large saucepan. Cover with cold water and bring to a simmer over a medium heat. Cook for 6 mins, or until just tender. Drain and leave to steam dry.
- Toss the potatoes in the curry paste and oil and add to a well-oiled baking tray.
- Crush the potatoes with a potato masher and oven bake 25 minutes.

Top tip: If you are not a fan of coconut you can leave it out of the crumb and swap the coconut milk for cream.

Katsu chicken curry

I see lots of different katsu chicken curries sweeping the nation, but the addition of desiccated coconut to the crumb here really lifts this whole dish, bringing it to another level.

Press to plate

50 minutes

INGREDIENTS

For the sauce
1 tbsp rapeseed oil
2 cloves garlic, crushed
1 onion, finely diced
1 thumb-sized piece
   ginger, grated
1 tbsp tomato puree
1 tsp brown sugar
1 tbsp curry powder
1 tsp turmeric
1 tsp ground coriander
200ml chicken stock
1 tin coconut milk

For the chicken
4 chicken breasts
2 free-range eggs,
   whisked
200g plain flour
1 tbsp curry powder
150g panko breadcrumbs
100g desiccated coconut

METHOD

- Drizzle the rapeseed oil in a medium-sized heavy-based pan. Add the onion, garlic and ginger. Sauté until the onion is soft.
- Add the tomato puree and sugar and mix until sugar has dissolved. Sprinkle over the curry powder, turmeric and ground coriander, and toast the spices for a minute.
- Pour over the stock and coconut milk and simmer for 40 minutes while you make your chicken.
- You will need three shallow dishes: put the flour in one, beaten egg in the second, and breadcrumbs and desiccated coconut in the final dish.
- Get your chicken breast and give it a little bash with a rolling pin to help flatten it.
- Dip the chicken into the flour, then egg, then breadcrumbs and repeat for each breast.
- Place the chicken in an ovenproof dish and bake at 180°C fan for 30 minutes until the chicken is cooked through.
- Serve the curry sauce poured over boiled rice, mixed veg and place the chicken on top.

Both these shots were taken by Simon Walsh during one of our live cook-alongs. I love the way that although we are side by side mine and Lils' actions are mirroring each other.

Chapter Five

Top tip: Use a crust of bread to check if your oil is at the right temperature. If it is, it will float to the top.

Bubbly batter mixed cod

Press to plate

45 minutes

Fresh cod in a bubbly batter is always requested by my hubby Damien when he gets free rein over what's for dinner. When frying, I usually use a wok and make sure I'm in the kitchen alone to watch the hot oil with zero distractions. The fresh cod in the crisp batter is so worth the effort.

INGREDIENTS

300g self-raising flour
50g cornflour
1 tbsp turmeric
600ml sparkling water
2 tbsp seasoned flour (to toss the fish in before the batter)
Around 1 litre vegetable oil, for frying
400g fillet sustainable fresh and smoked cod, mixed

METHOD

- Combine the flour, cornflour and turmeric in a large bowl, season with salt and pepper.
- You will also need to dust the fish in a little flour, this helps the batter to stick.
- Gradually pour the sparkling water into the bowl, stirring with a wooden spoon until you have a smooth, lump-free batter. Leave to rest for 5 minutes while you heat the oil.
- To cook the fish, deep-fry it by heating 1 litre of oil in a deep saucepan or a wok. I always make sure I'm in the kitchen on my own for this, with no children running around, as hot oil is dangerous.
- Pat the fish dry with kitchen paper, then toss it in a little seasoned flour.
- Shake off any excess, then dip into the batter to coat it.
- Carefully lower each fillet into the hot oil and fry for 8 to 10 minutes until golden and crisp and floating along the top of the oil.
- Using a large slotted spoon, lift out the fish, drain on kitchen paper, then sprinkle with salt. Serve with chips, peas and a lemon wedge.

Easy salmon en croûte

We are cutting out the hassle in this version of salmon en croûte, which sometimes can be quite a complicated dish. Using classic flavours of garlic, butter and lemon, this is another instant midweek hit. The kids will also really enjoy getting into the kitchen and helping with these.

Press to plate

50 minutes

INGREDIENTS

2 sheets ready-rolled puff pastry
4 fresh salmon darnes, skinned and
   boneless

1 fresh lemon
50g butter
A bush of fresh parsley
2 egg yolks, beaten, for glazing
Salt and pepper to season

Top tip: You can swap the salmon for any white fish, like cod or hake.

METHOD

- Preheat the oven to 180°C fan and prepare a baking tray large enough to hold 4 salmon darnes.
- Unroll the pastry sheets and cut each into four pieces; place each salmon darne in the centre of a pastry quarter.
- Season well with salt and pepper.
- Make a garlic butter by crushing the garlic, chopping the parsley and mixing with the softened butter. Add the zest of a lemon and a good squeeze of lemon juice.
- Spread a thick layer of the lemon garlic butter on top of the salmon, then top with another quarter sheet of pastry.
- Tuck the top sheet around the salmon, squeezing the edges of the two sheets together and pressing the edges with a fork to seal the pastry.
- Brush the edges with a little egg yolk, and bake in the preheated oven for 40 minutes, until golden all over.

Baked hake in pesto and pine nut crust

Press to plate

25 minutes

This is one of the quickest dishes to put together if you fancy a tasty fishy dishy fast. Serve with a simple side salad and some buttery baby potatoes for the perfect meal in minutes.

INGREDIENTS

4 hake fillets
100g pine nuts
4 tbsp basil pesto (you can make your own on page 167)

METHOD

- Preheat oven to 180°C fan.
- Place the hake onto a lined baking tray.
- Spread 1 tablespoon of pesto onto each hake fillet.
- In a pestle and mortar crush the pine nuts; if you don't have one bash the nuts with a rolling pin in a large bowl.
- Top the hake fillets with a good sprinkle of crushed pine nuts.
- Oven bake for 15 to 20 minutes.

Top tip: Swap out the basil pesto for sun-dried tomato pesto and a little shaving of Parmesan cheese.

Top tip: Pan-fried prawns are also perfect for this quick and simple sauce.

Smoked cod in lemon pepper cream

Press to plate

30 minutes

This is another quick and easy way to serve your favourite fish. I'm using smoked cod but any fish or even chicken works with this quick and simple lemon pepper cream sauce.

INGREDIENTS

For the fish

4 pieces of smoked cod
A pinch of black pepper
1 tbsp grated lemon rind
1 tbsp butter

Creamy garlic butter lemon sauce

1 tbsp butter
1 tbsp rapeseed oil
2 large cloves of garlic, minced
Lashings of crushed black peppercorns
120ml chicken or veg stock
250ml fresh cream
Zest of 1 medium lemon
3 tbsp fresh lemon juice
1 tsp Dijon mustard
A bunch of fresh parsley
Season with salt and pepper

METHOD

- Preheat oven to 180°C fan.
- Pat dry the smoked cod, spread with butter and season with a pinch of black pepper and lemon rind.
- Arrange on a nonstick baking sheet and oven bake for 20 minutes.
- Meanwhile make your sauce: in a saucepan over a medium heat add the oil, melt the butter and stir in the garlic; cook until fragrant.
- Pour over the chicken stock, lemon zest, lemon juice, and mustard.
- Season with additional pepper to taste.
- Whisk the sauce until completely combined.
- Add fresh snipped parsley and cream, and simmer.
- Take out the cod when cooked and pour over the sauce.
- Serve with hot baked potatoes or freshly cooked tagliatelle and buttered peas.

King prawn in coconut crumb

This is fast becoming Lils' favourite way to eat and make prawns and her absolute favourite 'picky dinner', served with a simple marie rose dipping sauce and crunchy carrot and cucumber batons.

INGREDIENTS

200g fresh prawns, deveined and shelled
2 fresh free-range eggs, whisked

100g panko breadcrumbs
100g desiccated coconut
1 tbsp curry powder

METHOD

- Preheat oven to 180°C fan.
- Arrange two shallow dishes, one with the whisked egg and one with the breadcrumb and desiccated coconut. Add the curry powder to the breadcrumb.
- Dip each prawn in the egg and then fully coat in the crumb.
- Oven bake on a flat oiled baking tray for 25 minutes.

Top tip: Add some lime or lemon zest to the breadcrumbs for an extra zing.

Top tip: Use mixed wild grain rice for a bit of extra texture.

Tuna, avocado and rice salad

Press to plate

25 minutes

This is a delicious, no-fuss salad with plenty of personality. Perfect for a hot summer's evening in the garden when nobody is in the mood to be slogging away in the kitchen.

INGREDIENTS

400g long-grain rice
2 tbsp olive oil
2 tbsp balsamic vinegar
1 tbsp honey
1 tsp Dijon mustard
Salt and pepper to season
2 x 120g cans tuna, drained
1 avocado
200g cherry tomatoes
100g sweetcorn
50g feta
100g rocket
2 tbsp pine nuts

METHOD

- Rinse the rice under cold water. Tip into a saucepan, cover with water and bring to the boil.
- Reduce the heat and simmer for 15 minutes until cooked. Drain and allow to cool while you make your dressing.
- In a bowl combine the oil, vinegar, honey and Dijon mustard with some salt and pepper to season.
- Toast the pine nuts for 3 minutes over a gentle heat in a pan with a little oil.
- Peel the avocado, slice the tomatoes and cube the feta.
- Once the rice has cooled, mix with the dressing and all the remaining ingredients and season. Divide between plates, sit in the sun and devour.

Top tip: Feel like upping the veggie intake? Add some fresh broccoli florets to the pasta while it boils.

Creamy lemon and prawn pasta

Press to plate

25 minutes

This is another lightning-quick fish dish to have midweek, saving your sanity yet again in the kitchen!

INGREDIENTS

450g tagliatelle or
  spaghetti
1 tbsp rapeseed oil
450g prawns, peeled and
  deveined
4 tbsp butter
3 cloves garlic, crushed
½ tsp crushed chilli flakes
4 tbsp crème fraîche
A bunch of fresh snipped
  chives
50g freshly grated
  Parmesan, plus more
  for garnish
Salt and freshly ground
  black pepper
Lemon zest and fresh
  parsley

METHOD

- In a large pot of salted boiling water, cook pasta according to the package directions.
- In a large pan over medium heat, heat oil. Add prawns, butter, garlic and the crushed chilli flakes. Season with salt and pepper and cook until prawns are pink.
- In a large bowl mix together crème fraîche, Parmesan and chives.
- Season with salt and pepper.
- When pasta is cooked, use tongs to add it to the crème fraîche and Parmesan and mix together.
- Pour over the excess juice and garlic from the pan and toss to coat.
- Top with some extra Parmesan and a little shave of lemon zest and fresh parsley.

Tuna poke tacos

Tuna poke tacos are traditionally made with raw slices of tuna. We love the flavour combos of a poke taco but are not brave enough just yet to use raw tuna. Canned tuna is so handy and really compliments the flavours in this dish. And the kids will love rolling their own tacos.

Press to plate

25 minutes

INGREDIENTS
4 flour tortilla wraps
1 tin tuna
2 scallions, thinly sliced
1 tbsp sesame seeds
4 tbsp soy sauce
1 tbsp sesame oil
1 tbsp honey
½ tsp dried chilli
1 large avocado, peeled
    and sliced
Lime wedges

METHOD
- Drain your tuna and mix it with the scallions, sesame seeds, soy sauce, sesame oil, honey and chilli in a large bowl.
- Warm your wraps on a dry pan for a few seconds.
- Add the tuna mixture and avocado with a squeeze of lime juice to the wraps and roll up.
- Enjoy.

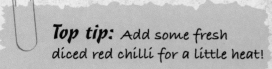

Top tip: Add some fresh diced red chilli for a little heat!

Top tip: Fresh salmon works also. Just drizzle with a little oil, add a dash of soy sauce and cook for 15 to 20 minutes.

Hot smoked salmon on a bed of stir-fried noodles

Hot smoked salmon can be eaten hot or cold. It works really well in this dish slightly warmed in the oven. We are upping the speed using straight-to-wok noodles as this is the perfect family meal if you just have come in from the training pitch and are starving.

INGREDIENTS

4 hot smoked salmon darnes
4 nests of straight-to-wok noodles
2 garlic cloves
1 onion
1 red pepper
1 tbsp sesame oil
2 tbsp soy sauce
2 tbsp honey

METHOD

- Place the salmon onto a lined baking tin and warm the hot smoked salmon for 10 minutes in the oven at 180°C fan.
- Slice veggies and crush garlic; stir-fry over a high heat in a little rapeseed oil or sesame oil for 5 minutes.
- Add the noodles straight to the wok and stir-fry for another minute, breaking up the noodles.
- Pour over honey and soy and give a good mix.
- Serve immediately with salmon on top. Perfect for busy days!

Top tip: Add a simple fried egg on top of your boxty dish for the breakfast of champions.

Fermanagh boxty and smoked salmon

Press to plate

30 minutes

This is a great dish to use up leftover mashed potato. Boxty is a traditional Irish country dish. In my home county of Fermanagh, it is mainly eaten around Halloween but, honestly, these little potato cakes are perfect for the whole family all year around.

INGREDIENTS

250g potatoes, peeled, cooked and mashed (or leftover mashed potato)
250g raw potatoes, peeled and grated
80g plain flour
100ml milk
1 egg, beaten
Salt and freshly ground black pepper
1–2 tbsp vegetable oil
A knob of butter
8 slices of smoked salmon
150ml sour cream
A bunch of fresh snipped chives
Lemon wedges to serve

METHOD

- Put both the mashed and grated potatoes in a bowl. Sprinkle over the flour and seasoning and mix until evenly combined.
- Add the milk, little by little, and mix until you have a thick batter. Stir in the beaten egg.
- Heat a little oil in a non-stick frying pan over a medium heat. Add a knob of butter. When the butter begins to foam, spoon a tablespoon of the mixture into the frying pan.
- Cook for a couple of minutes on each side until golden brown.
- Remove from the pan and keep warm while you finish cooking the rest of the potato pancakes.
- Serve with sliced smoked salmon, a spoon of soured cream and some snipped chives.

Jolene's Signature Dish

'Throw and go' slow-cooker chicken curry

I think everyone on the planet needs a good 'throw and go' slow-cooker curry in their weekly cooking repertoire. This is a great recipe for busy mornings when you just don't have the time to sauté the onion and red pepper on the pan. By using frozen veg you can literally throw it all into the slow cooker and go!.

INGREDIENTS

100g frozen diced onions
100g frozen diced peppers
3 free-range chicken breasts, diced
1 x 150g can of tomato puree
1 x 400mls can coconut milk
1 tbsp mango chutney
2 tbsp curry powder (mild or medium)
1 tsp garam masala
1 tsp ground cumin

METHOD

- Exactly what it says in the title: throw all the ingredients into your slow cooker and mix.
- Put the lid on and set the slow cooker or timing plug to cook for 2.5–3 hours on high or 4–5 hours on low, depending on your own device.
- I have been told that parents are actually buying slow cookers because they have discovered this recipe.

Top tip: A timing plug is a lifesaver for any slow cooker. Just set the allocated time on the plug and the slow cooker will come on at the right time for dinner to be ready when you arrive home. When the lid is on the device the food is kept warm and you are met with a steaming hot bowl of deliciousness after a busy day running around.

We are making our garlic bread from page 159 in this shot. As you can see, Lils is cracking up laughing. I think it's most likely the worst Peter Kay impersonation of all time by me that's making her laugh; it can't be helped though when making garlic bread.

Chapter Six

One-Pot Wash-Up

Easter lamb tray bake

Press to plate

50 minutes

Once spring has finally sprung, we can start putting a few lighter, fresher dishes onto the meal plan. My lamb chop tray bake is filled with all the colours of the rainbow, uniting the flavours of roasted butternut squash, simple parsley and rosemary with the classic Irish lamb chop.

INGREDIENTS

1 tbsp rapeseed oil
2 garlic cloves
1 red pepper
1 yellow pepper
1 butternut squash
6 baby potatoes
1 courgette
1 red onion
4 lamb chops
1 tbsp parsley
1 tbsp rosemary
Salt and freshly ground
   black pepper to season

METHOD

- Heat oven to 200°C fan.
- Crush garlic, peel and dice butternut squash, slice the pepper and courgette, half the baby potatoes and cut the red onion into wedges.
- Scatter all the vegetables on a large baking tray.
- Chop and sprinkle over the herbs, drizzle with oil and season.
- Place on the middle shelf of the oven and roast for 30 minutes.
- After 30 minutes, give the veggies a good shake and put them to one side of the tray.
- Season the lamb chops with a little salt and pepper (no need to oil them as they will release enough oil while cooking). Place them on the tray beside the veggies and return to the oven for 20 minutes (turning them after 10).
- Garnish with another sprinkle of fresh rosemary and parsley and serve with some leafy greens.

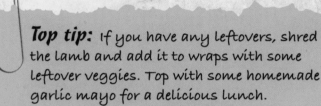

Top tip: If you have any leftovers, shred the lamb and add it to wraps with some leftover veggies. Top with some homemade garlic mayo for a delicious lunch.

107

Top tip: You can go alcohol-free here and just use a pint of stock instead of Guinness.

Paddy's Day beef and potato stew with dumplings

Press to plate

5 hours

This is everything you will ever need on St Patrick's Day, all in one pot.
Stew – check. Spuds – check. Guinness – check.
You just need to pop it on in the morning and let it simmer away while you watch the parade.

INGREDIENTS

500g stewing beef
1 tbsp flour (seasoned with salt and pepper)
2 onions
2 carrots
2 celery stalks
200g baby potatoes
1 beef stock cube mixed with 1 pint boiling water
Or ½ pint of stock mixed with ½ pint of Guinness
1 bunch fresh herbs: rosemary, parsley and thyme

For the herby dumplings
140g cold butter, diced
250g self-raising flour
100ml water
2 tbsp chopped mixed herbs

METHOD

- Cover the beef in seasoned flour. Heat a pan with oil and brown your beef in two batches. Leave to one side.
- Peel and chop the carrots, onions and celery. Add some oil to your saucepan and soften the prepared vegetables.
- Add the potatoes and season with a little salt and pepper.
- Put the beef back in and give a good mix. Pour in the stock, and Guinness if using, and let it bubble for a minute.
- Chop your lovely fresh herbs, leaving some aside for your dumplings
- Put the lid on the saucepan, turn to a low heat on the hob and simmer for around 4 hours (the longer the stew cooks the better).
- When the beef has broken down and tenderised, sprinkle with more fresh thyme, rosemary and parsley.
- Make your dumplings by rubbing the butter and flour together with your fingertips.
- Pour in water to bring them together and add the mixed herbs.
- Flour your hands and roll the mixture into golf-balls-sized balls.
- Place the dumplings on top of the stew and simmer for 20 minutes more until the dumplings are cooked through.

Top tip: Use the lid of your saucepan as a stencil when cutting your pastry to get the exact measurements for your dish.

One-pot chicken and smoked bacon pie

Press to plate

60 minutes

A chicken pie is the ultimate in comfort food and it's such a bonus when it can be cooked all in one pot. You will need a large Dutch oven or saucepan with a lid that can be used on the hob and in the oven.

INGREDIENTS

4 chicken breasts, diced
6 smoked bacon rashers, diced, fat cut off
2 garlic cloves, crushed
100g sweetcorn (or frozen peas)
1 heaped tbsp plain flour
½ pint hot chicken stock
½ pint milk
1 tsp Dijon mustard
1 tsp ground nutmeg
1 pack puff pastry

METHOD

- Preheat oven to 180°C fan.
- Place the Dutch oven over a medium heat with a glug of rapeseed oil. Seal chicken and bacon for 5 minutes in the oil then add the crushed garlic and season with a little salt and pepper.
- Add the corn (it can be frozen or from a can).
- Sprinkle over the flour to soak up all those lovely juices, and give a good mix.
- Pour over the liquid ¼ pint at a time, mixing each time you add more.
- Add a teaspoon of Dijon mustard and nutmeg and give another mix.
- Roll out the puff pastry and cut out a circle that will fit over your pot, using the lid as guide.
- Place the puff pastry on top of your mixture and finish with a little egg wash (egg mixed with a little water) brushed on top.
- Oven bake for 40 minutes until golden brown.

Top tip: If you don't own a risotto pan, I find a wok works just as well.

One-pan butternut squash risotto

Press to plate

45 minutes

The secret to a good risotto is giving the stock time to absorb before ladling in more. This butternut squash and mushroom risotto is such a tasty one-pot veggie meal option, and well worth taking the time to get it right.

INGREDIENTS

1 tbsp unsalted butter
1 tbsp rapeseed oil
200g risotto rice
2 garlic cloves, crushed
1 red onion, sliced
½ butternut squash, diced
200g button mushrooms, sliced
1 pint hot vegetable stock
100g grated Parmesan cheese
A small bunch of fresh thyme
A little drizzle of truffle oil

METHOD

- In a large pan add butter and oil. Fry the mushrooms until the moisture has evaporated, about 6 minutes.
- Add onion, garlic and diced butternut squash and fry for 5 minutes.
- Sprinkle in risotto rice and toast it for a minute.
- Ladle the hot vegetable stock into the rice two ladles at a time, stirring each time you add, letting the stock absorb into the rice each time. This takes around 20 minutes.
- When the stock has all been absorbed grate over the Parmesan.
- Sprinkle over a small bunch of fresh thyme leaves and finish with a drizzle of truffle oil.

Top tip: Crack in 4 eggs and make it brunch!

Sausage and apple tray bake

Press to plate

40 minutes

This is such a handy weekend meal. Whack all the ingredients onto one tray, stick it in the oven and in 40 minutes a succulent sausage supper is on the table with only one tray to wash up!

INGREDIENTS

12 good-quality pork
   sausages
2 tbsp rapeseed oil
1 tbsp honey
4 garlic cloves
1 large Pink Lady apple
1 onion, cut into quarters
2 carrots
1 tbsp chopped fresh
   rosemary and parsley
500g baby new potatoes
   (microwave-in-the-bag
   ones)
Salt and freshly ground
   black pepper

METHOD

- Preheat oven to 180°C fan and line a large baking tray with greaseproof paper.
- Microwave the baby potatoes according to the packet.
- Prepare your vegetables by peeling the onions and carrots. Slice the onions into wedges, and the carrots into 4-centimetre sticks. Core and wedge your apple also.
- With the back of your knife bruise each garlic clove, leaving the skin on.
- Slice the microwaved baby potatoes into halves and arrange on the baking tray with the garlic, vegetables and apple.
- Add your sausages to the tray, making sure they are scattered and not covered by any vegetables or apple.
- Drizzle with oil and honey and sprinkle with chopped fresh rosemary and parsley.
- Season with a little salt and pepper and oven bake for 35–45 minutes, until your sausages are golden brown and vegetables are cooked through.
- Squeeze a little roasted garlic over the potatoes to finish.
- Serve with a simple leafy salad.

Top tip: Add half broccoli and half cauliflower to up the veggie intake.

One-pot mac and cauliflower cheese

Press to plate

20 minutes

This is another perfect dish if the kids have had a day of afterschool activities or sports and you need something good on the table fast - added bonus is they will hardly even spot the cauliflower.

INGREDIENTS

400g macaroni pasta
1 small to medium head cauliflower, roughly chopped
1 tbsp butter
1 tbsp flour
1 pint whole milk
1 tsp Dijon mustard
1 tsp nutmeg (and a pinch to scatter on top at the end)
200g mixed grated cheddar and mozzarella
A handful of fresh snipped chives, to finish

METHOD

- Slice cauliflower into florets.
- Add the cauliflower to a pot of boiling water with the pasta, giving it a little stir so it doesn't stick to the bottom.
- Boil for 10 to 12 minutes, until pasta and cauliflower are cooked.
- Drain with a colander, and put back on the heat.
- Add a tablespoon of butter to the pasta and cauliflower, giving a good stir. Then add your flour, stirring and letting it cook out for a minute.
- Pour the milk in quarter by quarter, mixing each time you add it.
- When your sauce is nice and thick, add the Dijon mustard and nutmeg.
- Sprinkle in the cheddar and mozzarella, stirring while it melts into the sauce.
- Finish with some snipped chives and another sprinkle of nutmeg.
- Serve and enjoy – a huge hug in a bowl.

Top tip: Mix sliced sweet potatoes in with your baby potato topping for a bit of variety.

One-pot sausage hotpot

On a cold, blustery winter's evening, this is the one dish that will appeal to me. It's so wholesome, like a huge hug after a cold day.

Press to plate

50 minutes

INGREDIENTS

8 high-pork-content sausages
1 red onion, sliced
1 carrot, diced
1 garlic clove, crushed
1 tbsp flour
400ml beef stock
1 tsp Dijon mustard
A few splashes of Worcestershire sauce
Chopped fresh parsley
400g sliced baby potatoes, skin on

METHOD

- Slice the sausages in half and fry over a medium heat in a little oil until golden.
- Add onion and garlic, frying for a minute until soft.
- Add diced carrot and sprinkle in a tablespoon of flour.
- Add hot stock, quarter by quarter, stirring as you add.
- Dollop in Dijon mustard and a few splashes of Worcestershire sauce.
- Sprinkle in fresh chopped parsley.
- Top with sliced baby potatoes.
- Cover and oven bake at 180°C fan for 40 minutes.
- Crisp up potatoes under the grill for a minute before serving.

Top tip: This also makes the most tasty pie filling. Add a puff pastry hat and you have another delicious pie for your recipe collection.

One-pot country chicken and potato stew

Press to plate

40 minutes

This dish tastes so country that it should have a Stetson on top! This is one of those recipes that is so wholesome, one bowl is never enough.

INGREDIENTS

A glug of rapeseed oil
4 chicken breasts
1 tbsp plain flour
1 pint chicken stock
2 garlic cloves
1 medium onion
2 medium carrots
2 sticks of celery
200g baby potatoes
1 tsp wholegrain mustard
2 bay leaves
2 sprigs fresh thyme
1 bunch of fresh parsley

METHOD

• Crush the garlic, dice your chicken breasts, and peel and chop the veg.
• Put a saucepan over a medium heat with the rapeseed oil and soften your onion and garlic for 5 minutes.
• Add your carrot and celery and potato, giving them a good mix, and cook for another 2 minutes.
• Toss in the diced chicken breast, sealing them for about 2 minutes.
• Sprinkle over a good heaped tablespoon of flour and mix in well until it has soaked up all the lovely juices in the pan.
• Chop your fresh herbs and add them to the mix.
• Slowly pour in the chicken stock, quarter by quarter, mixing well.
• Chuck in your bay leaves and add the mustard.
• Cover with a lid and simmer for 30 minutes.

Top tip: Leftovers always taste even better the next day, filled deep in tortilla wraps with guacamole.

Cajun steak strip rice

Cajun steak strip rice is another delicious midweek meal when you are stuck for time and on the run. Add some diced chorizo, if you have it, for an extra flavour punch.

Press to plate

45 minutes

INGREDIENTS

4 sliced minute steaks
2 garlic cloves, crushed
1 white onion, chopped
2 celery stalks, chopped
1 red pepper, chopped
350g easy-cook long grain
   rice
600ml chicken stock
1 heaped tsp smoked
   paprika
1 tbsp Cajun seasoning
1 tbsp sundried tomato
   pesto
1 tbsp rapeseed oil
Salt and pepper to season
A sprinkle of cheddar
   cheese, to top

METHOD

- Over a high heat, fry off the garlic and onion in the olive oil.
- Add the chopped celery stalks and red pepper.
- Add the steak slices and cook them off in the pot until brown and crispy, stirring as you fry.
- Sprinkle over the smoked paprika and Cajun seasoning, then stir in your dollop of tomato pesto.
- Add in the easy-cook rice. Give all the ingredients a good mix together then pour in the chicken stock.
- Season with salt and pepper.
- Cover the pot with a lid and reduce the heat to a very low simmer for 25–30 minutes until the rice is cooked. Add in more liquid if needed.
- Give the dish one final mix then serve with a sprinkle of cheddar cheese on top.

Top tip: If you are not a fan of dried tagliatelle, just add 400g of fresh pasta and let it bubble for 5 minutes before serving.

One-pot pasta Bolognese

We all love a good pasta Bolognese. It's even better when it's cooked in 40 minutes and you've only got one pot to wash up!

Press to plate

40 minutes

INGREDIENTS

500g minced beef
3 cloves of garlic, crushed
1 onion, diced
1 red pepper, diced
3 tbsp tomato puree
A pinch of sugar
200ml passata
1 tbsp oregano
1 pint hot chicken stock
4 tagliatelle nests
A sprinkle of Parmesan
    and some basil leaves,
    to garnish

METHOD

- Over a medium heat with a drizzle of rapeseed oil soften onion and garlic.
- Add mince, browning it and breaking it up with a fork.
- Add diced red pepper and simmer for a minute.
- Dollop over tomato puree and mix in a sprinkle of sugar.
- Add passata and stock.
- Stir and throw in 4 tagliatelle nests, put on the lid and simmer for 5 minutes.
- After 5 minutes, tease out the tagliatelle with a fork, and simmer with the lid on for 30 minutes.
- Finish with Parmesan and fresh basil.

Happiness is the smell of freshly baked bread out of the oven! Lils' loaf recipe is on page 153 in our Kids in the Kitchen chapter. This is the perfect starter bread to get little hands busy in the kitchen. You can see the sense of pride written all over her face.

Chapter Seven

Simply Slow Cooking

Top tip: My Chinese peanut sauce from page 75 also works really well poured over the top of the pork fillet.

Chinese pulled pork

Pork fillet is one of those cuts of meat that works so well in the slow cooker. It is sweet and so tender and juicy, and takes on the Chinese flavours so well.

INGREDIENTS

500g pork fillet
1 tsp cornflour
2 tsp cold water

Sauce
3 tbsp soy sauce
3 tbsp honey
2 tbsp oyster sauce
1 tbsp rice wine vinegar
1 tsp Chinese 5 spice
2 garlic cloves, peeled and
  grated

METHOD

- Turn your slow cooker onto low and mix the sauce ingredients together in a small bowl.
- Add the pork fillet to the slow cooker and pour the sauce on top.
- Leave to cook for 2.5–3 hours on high or 5.5–6 hours on low.
- Remove the pork fillet and shred with two forks.
- Transfer the sauce from the slow cooker to a saucepan and bubble it over a high heat.
- Thicken the sauce with a cornflour paste of 1 tsp cornflour mixed with 2 tsp cold water.
- Strain the sauce to remove any fatty bits and pour over your pork fillet.

Barbecue slow cooker ribs

Barbecue meaty ribs are always a crowd pleaser. By slow-cooking them, they are hassle-free and so delicious and tender the meat is practically falling off the bone. The perfect family feast.

INGREDIENTS

1½ kg meaty pork ribs
300g barbecue sauce or make your own from page 6
800ml beef stock made with a stock pot
2 bay leaves

METHOD

- Put 4 tablespoons of barbecue sauce along with the rest of the ingredients into your slow cooker.
- Top up with the beef stock and slow cook on low for 8 hours until tender.
- Heat the oven to 200°C fan. Remove the ribs from the slow cooker using a slotted spoon.
- Add a drizzle of oil to an ovenproof dish and place the ribs on it.
- Cover with the remaining barbecue sauce.
- Oven bake for 20–30 minutes until they are starting to crisp on the outside.
- Alternatively, finish in a barbecue-proof silver tray over the barbeque on a sunny day.

Top tip: These also taste great in a honey and mustard glaze. Replace the barbecue sauce with 6 tablespoons of honey mixed with 3 tablespoons of Dijon mustard. Put half the sauce into the slow cooker with the meat and reserve half to spread over the ribs before placing them in the oven.

Top tip: Save some leftovers to make my epic turkey and ham pie on page 183.

Christmas turkey and ham

I remember having this idea for a hassle-free Christmas dinner using a large turkey breast and small ham joint and cooking them together in the slow cooker. It's one of my most popular recipes to date and I've been cooking Christmas dinner this way ever since.

INGREDIENTS

1 medium white onion
1 chicken stock cube or
    stockpot
500g–900g turkey breast
    joint
700g unsmoked Gammon
    joint

Optional ham glaze
3 tbsp runny honey
1 tbsp Dijon mustard

Gravy
Juices from your cooked
    meat
2 tsp cornflour
A dribble of cold water

METHOD

- Peel and chop your onion and place it in the bottom of your slow cooker.
- Add a chicken stock cube or stockpot. There is no need to add any liquid as both joints of meat will release around a pint of liquid during the slow cooking; this will make an amazing gravy.
- Cook on low for 8 hours/medium for 6 hours/high for 4 hours (this is a guideline as all slow cookers vary so check the turkey breast is pure white with no pink before serving and juices run clear).

Ham glaze (optional)
- 3 tablespoons of runny honey mixed with 1 tablespoon of Dijon mustard. Brush your cooked ham with the glaze and pop it in the oven at 180°C fan for 20 minutes until sticky and golden.

For the gravy
- Strain the juices from your slow cooker into a saucepan, gently heat, and when bubbling add a cornflour paste (2 teaspoons of cornflour mixed with a dribble of cold water) and whisk until thick.

Top tip: Pork mince also works really well in this dish.

Mozzarella, turkey and bacon meatballs

This is another delicious way to use up that pack of turkey mince we always seem to have sitting in the back of the freezer.

INGREDIENTS

For the meatballs

400g turkey mince
100g bacon lardons
1 good-quality mozzarella
    ball
2 scallions, sliced finely
1 garlic clove, crushed
1 tsp cumin
1 tsp oregano
1 tsp smoked paprika
A pinch of chilli

The sauce

400g tomato passata
100ml chicken stock
100g bacon lardons
1 small onion or shallot,
    finely chopped
1 red pepper
1 garlic clove, crushed
1 tsp dried chilli
1 tbsp oregano
1 tsp smoked paprika
Salt and pepper to season
A pinch of sugar
100ml cream, to finish

METHOD

- Make your meatballs by adding all your ingredients, except the mozzarella, to a large mixing bowl.
- Get your hands into the bowl and give it a good mix.
- Slice mozzarella into 9 cubes.
- Make 9 mini-meatballs and push a mozzarella cube into the centre of each meatball.
- Leave to one side while you make your sauce: add a drizzle of oil to a pan over a medium heat on the hob.
- Fry your diced onion, crushed garlic and bacon lardons.
- Pour over the passata and stock.
- Add the chilli, paprika and oregano.
- Season with salt and pepper and add a pinch of sugar, if you wish, to offset the acidity in the tomatoes.
- Add your meatballs to the slow cooker and pour your sauce over them.
- Cook on high for 4 hours or low for 8 hours.
- When cooked finish with a dash of cream.

Top tip: Add some extra zing by replacing the orange juice with a freshly squeezed lime.

Salmon teriyaki

This is such a tasty Japanese-style dish. The straight-to-wok noodles and tenderstem broccoli are such a handy addition to the slow cooker.

INGREDIENTS

4 salmon fillets, skin removed
4 nests of straight-to-wok noodles
200g tenderstem broccoli

For the sauce
4 tbsp soy sauce
1 tbsp rice wine vinegar
100ml fresh orange juice
100g brown sugar
1 tbsp oyster sauce
1 tsp Chinese 5 spice

METHOD

- Remove and discard skin from fish.
- Mix all the ingredients for your sauce in a mixing bowl.
- Add the salmon to your slow cooker.
- Pour over half the sauce, reserving the rest for serving.
- Cook for 3 hours on high or 7 hours on low.
- An hour before serving add the tenderstem broccoli and straight-to-wok noodles to the slow cooker and gently heat the remaining sauce on the hob.
- Serve by adding the noodles and broccoli to the plate first, placing the salmon on top.
- Finish with a drizzle of sauce.

Chinese shredded chicken soup

Everyone needs a good chicken soup recipe. This is perfect if you're feeling unwell as it's full of wholesome goodness with minimum effort.

INGREDIENTS

3 free-range chicken breasts
2 garlic cloves, crushed
100g tinned sweetcorn
1 tbsp soy sauce
2 bay leaves
1 bunch of fresh chopped chives
1 litre hot chicken stock
Cornflour paste to thicken: 1 tsp of cornflour mixed a dribble of water

METHOD

- To the slow cooker add garlic, sweetcorn and fresh snipped chives.
- Sit your chicken breasts on top with the bay leaves.
- Pour over the chicken stock and soy sauce.
- Add your cornflour paste and stir.
- Put the lid on and cook for 2.5–3 hours on high or 5.5–6 hours on low.
- When cooked, shred the chicken with two forks and add it back into the slow cooker.
- Serve with crusty bread rolls.

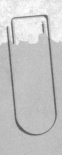

Top tip: To make a Chinese chicken noodle soup, when you remove the chicken breasts, add 4 nests of straight-to-wok noodles to the chicken broth, breaking up with a fork, and put the lid back on your slow cooker for 5 minutes while you shred the chicken. The heat of the broth will cook the noodles. Add the chicken back in and give a good mix. Serve with a shake of chilli flakes to up the heat a notch.

Top tip: This also makes a delicious pie filling. Simply transfer to an ovenproof dish and top with ready-rolled puff pastry then oven bake at 180°C fan for 40 minutes.

Epic beef rib steak

If you're looking for the ultimate in comfort food, this dish is the one for you. You can pick up the beef rib in your local butcher, season it and give it a little rub with rapeseed oil then seal it on a hot pan to colour it and lock in the flavour. Leave it to rest in the slow cooker while you caramelize the onion.

INGREDIENTS

500g rib of beef
1 white onion, diced
2 garlic cloves, crushed
1 carrot, diced
1 beef stock pot
A handful of fresh herbs, such as parsley, thyme, sage, rosemary or chive (pick 2 or 3), chopped
1 bay leaf
1 splash of Worcestershire sauce
1 pint hot water

METHOD

- Start by trimming any fat off your beef rib.
- Place a large pan on the hob over a medium heat with a drizzle of rapeseed oil, seal the beef and place it into the slow cooker to rest while you get some colour on your onion.
- Add the onion, crushed garlic cloves and carrot to the pan and sauté for around 5 minutes, then add to the slow cooker.
- Add the beef stock pot, fresh herbs and Worcestershire sauce to the slow cooker and give a good mix.
- Added a bay leaf and cover with water.
- Place the lid on your slow cooker and cook for 8 hours on low or 5 on high.
- You can also cook this dish on the hob on a simmer for 4 to 5 hours (the longer the better).
- When cooked, you can thicken the gravy if desired with a little cornflour paste (1 tsp cornflour mixed with 2 tsp cold water).
- I honestly don't say epic lightly.

Top tip: Use up any leftover ham by making our quick and easy jambons on page 186.

Honey, apple and pecan ham

This is such a simple way to add some extra-sweet honey and mustard flavour to a plain bacon joint. The sliced apple and pecan are the perfect accompaniment to the sweet juicy ham.

INGREDIENTS

700g unsmoked bacon joint
2 apples, sliced
100g pecan nuts
3 tbsp honey
1 tsp Dijon mustard
5 cloves

METHOD

- Mix the honey with the mustard.
- Add the bacon to the slow cooker and brush with the honey mustard mix.
- Drizzle a little more over, reserving some for serving.
- Add the pecan nuts and apple, and stud the fat of the bacon with the cloves.
- Cook on low for 4 hours.
- Slice and serve with boiled cabbage and mash.

Top tip: This also makes a delicious lasagne filling if you fancy a change from mince.

Beef ragu

Our slow-cooker beef ragu has all the flavours of your favourite Bolognese with the luxury of melt-in-the-mouth beef pieces.

INGREDIENTS

800g lean beef pieces
1 onion, diced
2 cloves garlic, crushed
2 celery stalks, sliced
2 carrots, diced
140g tomato paste
1 tbsp oregano
1 bay leaf
800g plum tomatoes
Pinch of brown sugar
200ml chicken stock
50g Parmesan

METHOD

- In a large pan with a drizzle of rapeseed oil brown the beef in batches, then add to your slow cooker.
- Drizzle the pan again with rapeseed oil and fry off the onion and garlic until softened.
- Add the diced carrot and celery to the pan to get a little colour on them. This will add a great depth of flavour to the overall dish.
- Add the veggies to the beef in the slow cooker and now just pour over the tomato paste and add a pinch of sugar and mix.
- Add the plum tomatoes and stock and sprinkle over the oregano.
- Add the bay leaf and grate in the Parmesan.
- With the lid on, cook on high for 6 hours or low for 8 hours, until the beef is tender and falling apart.

Top tip:
1: Oil the slow cooker first to prevent the rice from sticking.
2: Use boil-in-the-bag easy-cook rice.
3: Rinse the rice in a sieve before adding it to the slow cooker.

Golden veggie rice and chicken

This is such a handy, whack-it-all-into-the-slow-cooker kinda recipe. There are a few little pointers I would advise you to take to ensure you get perfect fluffy savoury rice every time. Once you do these, just put the lid on and forget about it.

INGREDIENTS

200g easy-cook rice
1 carrot, diced
100g sweetcorn
3 chicken breasts
1 tbsp soy sauce
1 chicken stock cube
1 tsp turmeric
800ml cold water
1 tbsp chicken seasoning
Crème fraîche and chives,
    to finish

METHOD

- Add a drizzle of oil to your slow cooker, rubbing it around the sides; this prevents the rice from sticking.
- Remove the rice from the bags and rinse under cold water.
- Add the rice to your slow cooker with the carrot and sweetcorn.
- Pour over the cold water and soy sauce, and add the turmeric and stock cube.
- Give a good mix.
- Add the chicken seasoning to the breasts and wrap the 3 chicken breasts in greaseproof paper.
- Place the wrapped chicken breasts on top.
- Put your lid on and cook for 3 hours on high.
- After 3 hours remove your chicken breasts and shred them, and also give your rice a good stir.
- Add the chicken back in and finish with crème fraîche and snipped fresh chives.

It's the little jobs that can be the most fun in the kitchen. If your child isn't quite ready for knife skills, there are loads of other age-appropriate jobs they can do instead, like peeling garlic and onions. Little jobs like these are a fantastic way to build fine motor skills and hand-eye coordination.

Chapter Eight

Kids in the Kitchen

MEATBALL MARINARA SUBS

This is one of our most popular kids-in-the-kitchen dishes from our cook-alongs with Lils.

INGREDIENTS

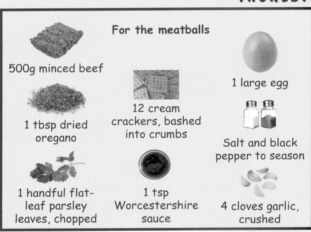

For the meatballs

500g minced beef

1 tbsp dried oregano

1 handful flat-leaf parsley leaves, chopped

12 cream crackers, bashed into crumbs

1 tsp Worcestershire sauce

1 large egg

Salt and black pepper to season

4 cloves garlic, crushed

For the 2-minute marinara sauce

1 tsp oregano

A pinch of sugar

Salt and freshly ground black pepper

2 tbsp tomato puree

200g shredded cheddar and mozzarella mix

4 crusty sub rolls or demi-baguettes

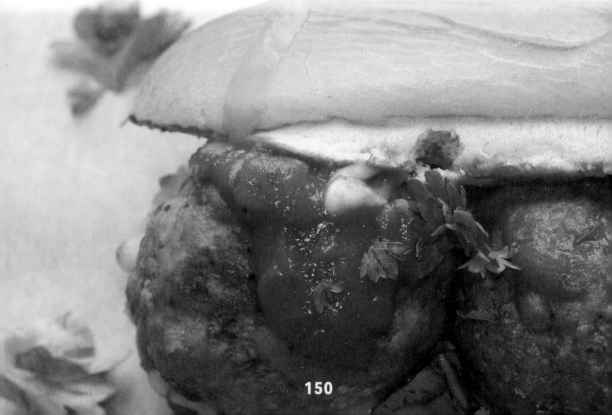

METHOD

1. Preheat the oven to 180°C fan.

2. Place mince in a large mixing bowl and punch a well into the centre of the meat. Fill well with the egg, crackers, garlic, Worcestershire sauce, parsley and oregano, and season with a little salt and pepper.

3. Mix up meatball ingredients until well combined.

4. Divide the mix into 4 equal parts, roll each part into 3 mini-balls and place in a mini-muffin tin or space equally on a non-stick baking sheet.

5. Place meatballs in the oven and cook for about 10–15 minutes.

6. Test the meatballs by breaking one open and making sure the meat is cooked through before removing from the oven.

7. Meanwhile, in a little bowl mix the tomato puree, oregano and a pinch of sugar together. Slice your rolls, keeping one side intact, press the bread down in the centre and spread with tomato sauce.

8. Top with shredded cheese and place subs in the oven for 2 minutes to melt cheese.

9. Remove from the oven and place 3 meatballs into each sub.

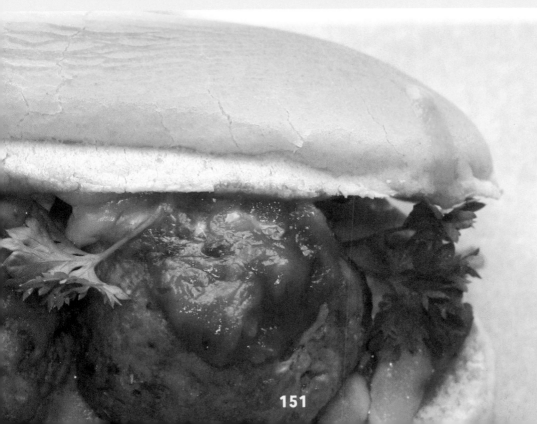

151

LILS' BROWN LOAF

Happiness is the smell of freshly baked bread! There is such a sense of achievement when you take your very own loaf of bread out of the oven. Fresh, homemade, delicious!

INGREDIENTS

220g coarse wholemeal flour

1 tsp bicarbonate of soda

1 tbsp melted butter

300ml milk

50g plain flour

15g of soft dark brown sugar

1 tbsp honey

METHOD

1. Preheat oven to 200°C fan.
2. Sift both flours into a large mixing bowl, add the remaining coarse wholemeal flour in the sieve to the bowl.
3. Sift in bicarbonate of soda (not baking powder or it won't rise).
4. Add soft brown sugar.
5. Make a well and pour in milk, melted butter and honey.
6. Mix together with a whisk.
7. Fill a lined 2lb loaf tin.
8. Oven bake at 200°C fan for 40 minutes.

PRESS PIZZA

The perfect pizza at any time for all ages! Kids just love getting hands-on with this recipe, rolling out the dough and choosing their own toppings. A guaranteed winner every time.

INGREDIENTS

For the dough

200g plain flour

A good pinch of salt

2 tbsp rapeseed oil

1 tbsp fast-action yeast

120ml warm water

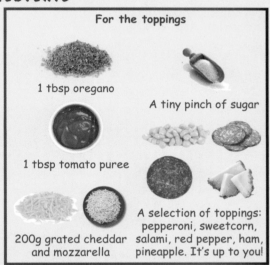

For the toppings

1 tbsp oregano

A tiny pinch of sugar

1 tbsp tomato puree

200g grated cheddar and mozzarella

A selection of toppings: pepperoni, sweetcorn, salami, red pepper, ham, pineapple. It's up to you!

METHOD

1. Preheat oven to 240°C fan.

2. In a large mixing bowl, add flour and salt and make a little well in the middle.

3. Pour the water, oil and fast-action yeast into the well and mix all together with a spoon.

4. Flour your hands and get them into the bowl and give a good knead.

5. Flour your work surface and give another good knead, stretching the dough to let the yeast do its magic.

6. Line your baking tray with greaseproof paper and roll out your dough to the same size as your tray.

7. Make your pizza sauce by mixing together the tomato puree, sugar and oregano.

8. Top dough with the pizza sauce.

9. Then scatter with cheese and add your favourite toppings.

10. Turn the oven down to 180°C fan before you put the pizza in.

11. Oven bake for 30 minutes, checking after 20 minutes.

12. Perfect pizza every time!

HIDDEN VEGGIE SAUSAGE ROLLS

This is a delicious way to get creative in the kitchen and to sneak some veggies in too! This recipe makes 8 rolls.

INGREDIENTS

 400g good-quality sausage meat

 1 tbsp tomato relish

 1 apple, peeled and grated

 1 courgette, peeled and grated

 1 carrot, peeled and grated

 1 garlic clove, crushed

 1 tbsp dried sage

 Salt and pepper to season

 320g puff pastry

 1 beaten egg for egg wash

 A sprinkle of poppy seeds or sesame seeds

METHOD

1. Preheat oven to 180°C fan.

2. Prepare a baking tray with greaseproof paper.

3. Peel and grate your apple and veg and peel and crush your garlic.

4. Get an adult to help you if needed to add the grated apple and veg to a pan with a drizzle of rapeseed oil; fry for 6 minutes until softened.

5. Drain the apple and veg in a sieve.

6. Add to a bowl and mix with the relish, sage and sausage meat.

7. Get your hands in and give a good mix.

8. Season with a little salt and pepper.

9. Cut the puff pastry into 8 rectangles.

10. Put your sausage and veg mix onto the edge of the pastry and roll up, sealing the edges with a fork.

11. Repeat 8 times.

12. Brush each one with a lightly beaten egg and sprinkle with some seeds.

13. Place onto a baking tray, spaced 2cm apart.

14. Bake in the oven for 30–40 minutes until pastry is golden.

GARLIC BREAD

Make your very own garlic bread. So simple but this tastes delicious on its own or teamed with our press pizza for your very own movie night feast.

INGREDIENTS

4 part-baked mini-baguettes

4 garlic cloves

A bunch of fresh parsley

100g butter, softened

80g cheddar cheese, grated

METHOD

1. Make the garlic butter by peeling and crushing the garlic cloves. An easy way to do this is with a fork.

2. Snip the fresh parsley and mix the garlic and parsley into the butter.

3. Cut the baguettes in half and spread on the garlic butter generously.

4. Sprinkle the grated cheddar on top then bake in the oven for 15 minutes.

PLEASE TRY IT SALAD

Ok we don't know many kids who love salad, but please give this one a try! It tastes better when you make it yourself...

INGREDIENTS

2 heads baby gem lettuce

50g croutons

50g grapes

50g sweetcorn

½ cucumber, diced

½ carrot, grated

1 tbsp mayonnaise or ranch dressing

METHOD

1. In a large mixing bowl cut up the baby gem lettuce with a scissors.
2. Mix in croutons and sweetcorn.
3. For younger children, slice the grapes lengthways into 5 pieces.
4. Peel the carrot and use the peeler to cut it into ribbons.
5. With adult supervision, slice the cucumber.
6. Add a tablespoon of mayo or ranch dressing.
7. Mix and serve.

TARTE FLAMBÉE

Fancy pizza but you have no yeast? No problem, this French-style pizza is the answer - a great recipe to let the kids get stuck into. And it's delicious paired with our Please Try It Salad.

INGREDIENTS

200g plain flour

2 tbsp rapeseed oil

120 ml warm water

A good pinch of salt

For the topping

2 tbsp crème fraîche

1 tsp nutmeg

200g grated Emmental

200g pancetta

METHOD

1. Preheat oven to 180°C fan.

2. In a large mixing bowl, add flour and salt and make a little well in the middle.

3. Add the water. Flour your hands and get them into the bowl and give a good knead.

4. Line your baking tray with greaseproof paper and roll out your dough to the same size as your tray.

5. Top dough with a spread of crème fraîche and a sprinkle of nutmeg.

6. Then scatter over the Emmental and pancetta.

7. Oven bake for 20 minutes.

PESTO ROSSO

Homemade pesto tastes so much better than the jar, you won't believe how easy it is to make yourself. This pesto is absolutely delicious simply stirred into pasta.

INGREDIENTS

4 tagliatelle nests

200g sundried tomatoes, drained

4 large roasted red peppers

2 tbsp tomato paste

50g Parmesan, grated

Pinch of sugar

1 tbsp oregano

2 fresh basil leaves

60g pine nuts

3 tbsp olive oil

METHOD

1. You may need an adult to help boil tagliatelle according to the packet instructions.

2. Also get some adult supervision for this bit: in a food processor or mini-chopper add the drained sundried tomatoes, roasted red peppers, tomato paste, oregano, fresh basil leaves and pine nuts, and blitz together until you have a paste.

3. Drizzle in the olive oil and blitz again. Season with salt and pepper.

4. Ask an adult to remove the blade. Then, with a silicone spatula remove the pesto and add to a bowl. Grate in the Parmesan and mix.

5. When pasta is cooked drain and add 3 good tablespoons of pesto to it.

6. Serve immediately with a little more Parmesan and a torn basil leaf.

BASIL PESTO

If you're more of a fan of green pesto, why not give this one a go? Delicious fresh basil, zingy lemon and creamy Parmesan cheese - you can put this pesto on just about anything!

INGREDIENTS

200g basil leaves

100g spinach leaves

100g Parmesan cheese, finely grated

100g pine nuts

2 cloves garlic

½ lemon, squeezed

4 tbsp olive oil

Salt and pepper to taste

METHOD

1. Get an adult to supervise with this bit: place all of the ingredients into a food processor or mini-chopper with 2 tablespoons of olive oil.

2. Blitz until smooth.

3. Scrape down the sides with a silicone spatula.

4. Add another 2 tablespoons of olive oil and blitz again.

5. Add a little water if the pesto looks dry.

6. Spoon over your favourite boiled pasta.

COWBOY PINWHEELS

You will have so much fun making your own cowboy pinwheels.
A really simple treat for the kids to enjoy.

INGREDIENTS

  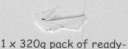

1 egg   200g diced ham   1 x 320g pack of ready-rolled puff pastry   1 tbsp barbecue sauce   150g smoked cheddar

METHOD

1. Preheat oven to 180°C fan.

2. Line a flat baking tray with baking paper and set aside.

3. Remove the pastry from the box and unroll onto a flat surface.

4. Spread barbecue sauce evenly over the entire pastry.

5. Scatter with grated smoked cheese.

6. Top with diced ham.

7. Roll the pastry into a log, like a Swiss roll.

8. Slice into 2cm pieces and place 2 cm apart, cut side up, on the baking tray.

9. Sprinkle with a little more cheese.

10. Brush with egg wash.

11. Bake for 30 minutes until golden and cheese is melted and bubbling.

Christmas is my favourite time of year to get into the kitchen, so much so I have dedicated this whole chapter to 'Season's Eatings'. Not only is it filled with the most delicious Christmas trimmings and sides, they all still have our quick-and-easy step-by-step flavour, which means less time at the stove and more time with the people who matter.

Chapter Nine

Season's Eatings

Top tip: Roll into 6 rounds and cook for 20 minutes to make spiced rock buns.

Warming spiced brown soda

This spiced soda bread is just delicious in the run-up to Christmas. Teamed with a hot mug of tea by the fire and topped with strawberry jam, it is just heavenly.

INGREDIENTS

50g unsalted butter, diced
150g plain flour
250g wholemeal flour,
    plus a little extra for
    dusting
15g soft dark brown sugar
1 tsp bicarbonate of soda
1½ tsp mixed spice
150g fruit mix
300ml buttermilk

METHOD

- Preheat the oven to 180°C fan.
- Start by sifting the flour and bicarbonate of soda into a large mixing bowl.
- Sprinkle in the wholemeal flour and add the unsalted diced butter.
- Rub the butter into the mix with your fingertips, until you have a fine breadcrumb texture.
- Stir in the mixed spice, fruit mix and the soft brown sugar.
- Pour over the buttermilk and quickly stir with a wooden spoon.
- Tip out onto a flour-dusted surface, flour your hands and gently bring the mixture together into a ball.
- Transfer to a flour-dusted baking sheet.
- Use a knife to score a cross on the top and bake for 40 minutes until it is crusty on the outside.
- Do not open the oven while it's baking.
- Check with a skewer and if it comes out clean that means it's cooked; leave to cool upside down in a damp tea towel.

Santa's chocolate chip cookies

Every year on Christmas Eve we make these cookies to leave out for Santa and they are always devoured. The big man himself has actually told me they are the best he's ever tasted.

INGREDIENTS

80g soft light brown sugar
80g caster sugar
100g unsalted butter, softened
1 medium free-range egg
275g plain flour
A pinch of baking powder
1 tsp vanilla essence
200g chocolate chips

METHOD

- Preheat oven to 180°C fan and line a flat baking tray with greaseproof paper.
- Make sure your butter is soft before you start.
- In a large bowl cream together the butter and sugars with a wooden spoon.
- Crack in your egg and mix again.
- Pour in the vanilla essence and mix.
- Add the flour and baking powder and give a good mix until you have a crumbly cookie dough.
- Stir in the chocolate chips.
- Roll into balls and flatten each one down slightly.
- Place on a baking tray in the centre of the oven and bake for around 15 minutes.
- Leave to cool for 10 minutes (they will harden as they cool).

Top tip: Add in white chocolate chips too. It's Christmas, go on!

Caramelised pecan sprouts

Long gone are the days of boring boiled Brussels sprouts at Christmas! By roasting them they are crunchy and sweet and work an absolute treat.

INGREDIENTS

20 Brussels sprouts
1 tbsp rapeseed oil
1 tbsp balsamic vinegar
1 tbsp brown sugar
50g pecan nuts
50g bacon bits (optional)

METHOD

- Preheat oven to 180°C fan.
- Half and peel the outer skin off your sprouts.
- Add to a lined baking tray with your pecan nuts and bacon bits.
- In a little bowl mix the rapeseed oil, balsamic vinegar and brown sugar, and add to the sprouts, mixing well.
- Oven bake for 30–40 minutes until your sprouts are caramelised and bacon is crispy.

Top tip: Add a little heat with a sprinkle of chilli flakes.

175

Top tip: Add some boiled pasta to any leftovers to make a delicious cheesy lunch.

Cauliflower and broccoli cheese

You won't believe it but the cauliflower and broccoli cheese is our Lils' favourite part of the Christmas dinner and once you try this, you won't be surprised to see why.

INGREDIENTS

1 cauliflower head
1 broccoli head
50g butter
4 tbsp flour
500ml milk
150g strong cheddar
   cheese, grated
1 tsp Dijon mustard
Salt and pepper to season
3 tbsp cheesy crackers,
   crushed, to top

METHOD

- Preheat oven to 180°C fan.
- Bring a large saucepan of water to the boil, then add the cauliflower and broccoli florets, parboiling for 6 minutes.
- Drain and then tip into an ovenproof dish. Put the saucepan back on the heat.
- Melt the butter and add the flour.
- Add the milk, quarter by quarter, whisking as you add.
- Whisk for 2 minutes while the sauce simmers and becomes nice and thick.
- Season with a little salt and pepper and add the mustard.
- Turn off the heat, stir in most of the grated cheddar cheese and pour over the cauliflower and broccoli.
- Scatter over the remaining cheese, top with 3 tablespoons of crushed crackers.
- Put in the bottom shelf of the oven and bake for 20 minutes until bubbling and oozing.

Top tip: Save some stuffing for your leftover pie; it really takes the flavour to another dimension.

Sage and sausage meat stuffing

I have been told this sausage meat stuffing is a meal in itself – the chopped walnuts and cranberries really take the flavour up a notch.

INGREDIENTS

8 Irish pork sausages
2 tbsp butter
100g breadcrumbs
½ white onion
1 tbsp dried sage
50g walnuts (optional)
50g dried cranberries
    (optional)

METHOD

- Preheat oven to 180°C fan.
- Remove the skin from the sausages.
- Dice the onion, chop the walnuts and cranberries in half.
- Combine all the ingredients in a large mixing bowl, getting your hands in to give it a good mix.
- Add to an ovenproof dish and cover with greaseproof paper or tinfoil.
- Oven bake for 30 minutes. Remove the foil/ greaseproof paper and mix, breaking up your stuffing into little chunks with a spoon, and put back into the oven for a further 10 minutes uncovered to crisp up the edges.

Top tip: Add any root vegetable to this dish; turnip, squash or sweet potato work really well.

Carrot and parsnip gratin

This is another way to make those sides a little extra special for the main event on Christmas Day.

INGREDIENTS

40g unsalted butter
1 tbsp rapeseed oil
2 shallots
5 parsnips
5 carrots
2 garlic cloves, crushed
2 bay leaves
2 fresh rosemary and
   thyme sprigs
1 tbsp flour
300ml vegetable/chicken
   stock
1 tsp wholegrain mustard
250g mascarpone
150g grated mozzarella
   and cheddar
50g panko breadcrumbs

METHOD

- Heat the oven to 180°C fan.
- Dice shallots and crush garlic.
- Peel and slice your carrots and parsnips into fine rounds.
- In a heavy-based ovenproof saucepan, like a Dutch oven, melt the butter and pour over the oil.
- Add the shallots and garlic and sauté for 5 minutes.
- Add parsnips, carrots, bay leaves and fresh rosemary and thyme leaves.
- Stir and sprinkle over the flour.
- Pour over the stock and add the mustard.
- Stir in the mascarpone and 100g of the grated cheese, reserving some to sprinkle at the end.
- Top with breadcrumbs and the reserved cheese, then bake for 35–40 minutes until golden.

Top tip: Having family over? This pie filling makes delicious vol au vents.

Leftover turkey and ham pie

I have been told this pie tastes even better than the main meal the day before. The stuffing really takes it to the next level.

INGREDIENTS

200g sliced leftover turkey
200g sliced leftover ham (fat cut off)
Leftover stuffing

For the sauce
1 tbsp butter
1 heaped tbsp plain flour
400ml chicken stock cube mixed with warm water
200ml milk
1 tsp Dijon mustard

Top with shop-bought ready-made puff pastry
Or simply make your own shortcrust (if you forgot to pick up pastry in the big Xmas shop):

Easy shortcrust pastry
225g plain flour
100g cold butter, diced
1–2 tbsp water
A little seasoning with salt and pepper

METHOD

Method for pastry
- Into a large mixing bowl sift the flour and add the diced butter.
- Bring the flour and butter together with your fingertips until you get a breadcrumb consistency.
- Add a tablespoon of water and bring together with your hands until you have a firm dough; add more water if needed.
- Give a little knead and roll into a ball, wrap in clingfilm and leave to rest in the fridge while you make your pie filling.

Method for the pie filling
- Preheat oven to 180°C fan.
- In a deep ovenproof dish arrange leftover turkey, ham and stuffing.
- In a saucepan make your sauce by melting butter over medium heat and whisking in a good heaped tablespoon of flour.
- Add the warm chicken stock quarter by quarter to the saucepan, whisking as you add it, letting it thicken each time.
- Top with milk, whisking while you let the sauce thicken.
- Add the mustard, stir and season with a little salt and pepper.
- Pour the sauce over your turkey, ham and stuffing in your pie dish.
- Top with pastry and brush with a beaten egg.
- Oven bake for 40 minutes until the pastry is golden.

Honey-glazed pigs in blankets

These make the perfect Christmas breakfast washed down with a little glass of Bucks Fizz. Sure go on, it's Christmas!

INGREDIENTS

16 good-quality cocktail sausages
2 tbsp honey
1 tsp Worcestershire sauce
12 thin smoked American-style bacon slices

METHOD

- Preheat the oven to 180°C fan.
- In some vegetable oil brown the sausages a little on the pan for 8 minutes (this step is optional if you like a little colour on your sausage).
- In a bowl, toss the sausages with honey and Worcestershire sauce until coated.
- Cover with a long piece of streaky bacon, winding it round until neatly wrapped.
- Arrange the bacon-wrapped sausages on a baking sheet.
- Roast for 30–35 minutes, until dark golden.

Top tip: Add these to your cheese board with cocktail sticks and watch the daddies of the house devour these before any selection of fancy cheeses.

Oozing oven-baked brie

The perfect starter for your Christmas Day dinner, served simply with cranberry sauce and crackers to dip into that oozing cheese.

INGREDIENTS

200g Brie, sliced into wedges

2 free-range eggs, whisked

200g cheesey crackers, whizzed to a crumb

METHOD

- Preheat oven to 180°C fan.
- Whizz up your crackers and add them to a bowl.
- Dip your Brie into the egg, completely covering it, and then in the cracker crumb.
- Do this process twice to completely cover the Brie.
- Place onto a lined baking tray.
- Oven bake for 8–10 minutes.

Top tip: Freeze the cheese overnight before cooking if you would like less ooze.

Use up the ham jambon

Who doesn't love a good jambon?! These are absolutely delicious and the perfect way to use up the leftover ham on the third day after Christmas.

INGREDIENTS

1 x 320g pack of puff pastry
1 x 250g pack Mascarpone cheese
1 tsp Dijon mustard

A sprinkle of grated nutmeg
100g cooked ham, diced
100g Mozzarella and cheddar mix (plus a
   little more to scatter on top)
1 egg yolk

Top tip: Add some cranberry sauce for that extra taste of Christmas.

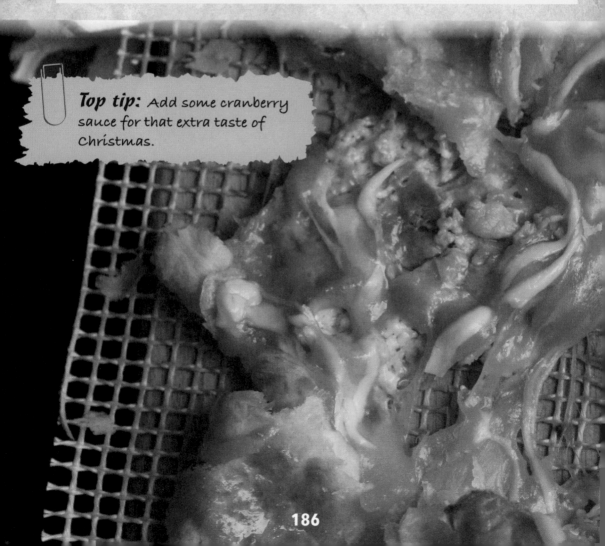

METHOD

- Preheat oven to 180°C fan.
- Roll out puff pastry and cut into 6 even rectangles.
- In a large mixing bowl mix together the mascarpone, Dijon mustard and nutmeg, with a wooden spoon.
- Dice your ham and add it to the bowl.
- Add the cheddar and Mozzarella mix.
- Dollop a good tablespoon of the cheese and ham mixture into the centre of each pastry rectangle.
- Fold in the corners to make little parcels.
- Brush with the egg yolk.
- Oven bake for 30 minutes.
- So tasty, hot or cold, and to grab and go!

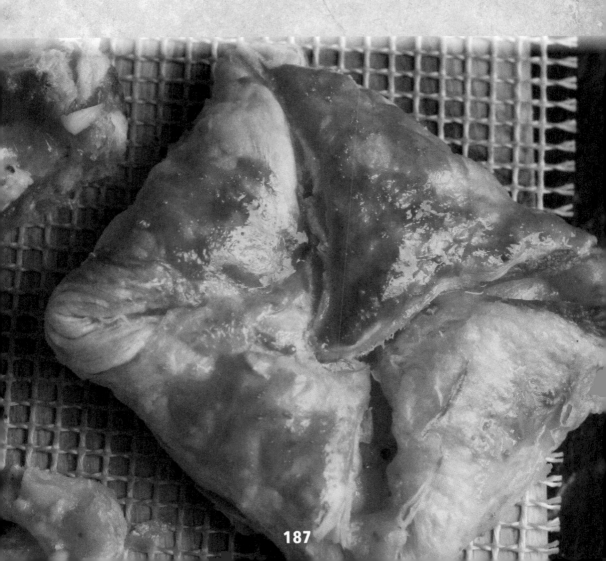

If you look close enough you may spot a smear of chocolate across my cheek. It's Christmas Eve in this photo, Christmas FM is blaring from the jukebox, and we are making Santa cookies from page 174.

Chapter Ten

Bake Together Treats

Top tip: Change the lemon to orange for delicious orange drizzle cake.

Lemon drizzle

This has to be one of mine and Lils' absolute favourite bake together treats! An absolute classic.

INGREDIENTS

210g self-raising flour
½ tsp baking powder
200g baking margarine,
   at room temperature
200g caster sugar
3 eggs
1 lemon
100g icing sugar
1tsp water

METHOD

- Preheat oven to 180°C fan.
- In a large bowl cream together margarine and sugar with a wooden spoon.
- When light and fluffy add eggs one at a time, mixing each time.
- Lift your sieve good and high and sift in the self-raising flour and baking powder.
- Mix with a wooden spoon to keep it light and fluffy.
- Juice and zest the lemon. Add in half the lemon juice and half the zest, reserving the rest for the icing.
- Add your batter to a fully lined 2lb loaf tin and oven bake for 40 minutes. Squeeze over a little more lemon juice when baked.
- When fully cooled drizzle with icing.
- To make the icing sift icing sugar and mix with a teaspoon of water. Add in the remainder of your lemon juice and zest. Drizzle over your loaf and leave for a minute for the icing to set before slicing.

Top tip: You can also add some eyebrows with liquorice laces and eyes with Smarties.

Easter bunny cupcakes

These cute little bunny cupcakes are a fantastic idea for an Easter bake together treat.

INGREDIENTS

For cupcake batter
120g self-raising flour
100g butter
100g caster sugar
2 eggs

For decoration
200g white chocolate
12 white marshmallows
12 chocolate chips
2 tbsp coloured sprinkles

METHOD

- Preheat oven to 180°C fan. Prepare a cupcake tin with cupcake cases.
- Measure all the ingredients for the cupcake batter into a large mixing bowl, cracking your eggs in last.
- Mix well with your wooden spoon.
- Add a tablespoon of cupcake batter into each cupcake case.
- Oven bake for 15 minutes.
- Meanwhile, melt white chocolate in a bowl over a saucepan of simmering water.
- Put coloured sprinkles onto a flat plate.
- Carefully cut 12 white marshmallows diagonally to make your bunny ears.
- Get a little helper to press the sticky side of the marshmallow into the sprinkles.
- Top each cupcake with a spoon of white chocolate.
- Stick two bunny ears onto each cupcake, using the melted chocolate as glue.
- Finish with a chocolate chip nose.

Rhubarb cake crumble

This is a great bake for an autumn desert when rhubarb is in season. Serve warm topped with vanilla ice cream or custard for a delicious warming treat.

INGREDIENTS

The crumble
60g unsalted butter, melted
120g plain flour
60g light brown sugar
A pinch of salt

The filling
200g rhubarb, cut into 1-inch pieces
2 tbsp light brown sugar
1 tbsp flour (this stops the rhubarb from sinking)

The sponge
120g self-raising flour
100g unsalted butter, room temperature
120g icing sugar
2 large eggs
1 vanilla pod
1 tsp water

Top tip: If you are not a fan of rhubarb, you can replace it with apples or even strawberries and raspberries.

METHOD

- Preheat oven to 160°C fan.
- Line an 8-inch square baking tray with baking paper and grease it with a little butter.
- Chop your rhubarb and place in a mixing bowl, mix it with the brown sugar and flour.
- To make your crumble, melt butter and add it to another mixing bowl with the sugar and a pinch of salt. Combine with a whisk.
- Add the flour little by little and mix with a fork until you have a large breadcrumb-like crumble. Put to one side until you need it.
- For the sponge, cream together butter and icing sugar with your electric hand mixer in a third mixing bowl. Mix for a couple of minutes until light and fluffy.
- Add eggs one by one and keep mixing.
- Sift in your self-raising flour and mix again.
- Scrap out the inside of your vanilla pod and mix again, adding a teaspoon of water.
- Pour in your cake mixture to the bottom of the baking tray, spreading it out to the edges for an even finish.
- Scatter the rhubarb over the sponge and finish by sprinkling your crumble mix on top.
- Oven bake for 40–45 minutes.
- Let cool a little before cutting into 12 rectangular bars. This is delicious served with vanilla ice-cream.

Top tip: The secret is to go low and slow with the caramel. Low heat, stir gently until it simmers, take it off the heat.

Caramel squares

My social media channels absolutely blow up any time we post about these caramel squares, and when you try them you will see why!

INGREDIENTS

For the base
18 digestive biscuits, crushed
120g melted butter

For the caramel
150g soft brown sugar
150g butter
1 can condensed milk

For the topping
200g good-quality chocolate

METHOD

- Crumb the digestives and add the melted butter.
- Mix together and press into a 20–22cm square lined tin, with a lip of at least 3cm.
- Leave to chill in the fridge.
- Melt together butter and sugar for the caramel, stirring with a silicone spatula. Once melted, let it simmer gently.
- Add your condensed milk and stir while you bring back to a gentle simmer. This can take up to 15 minutes. Use a low heat and keep stirring until it thickens and tiny bubbles appear.
- Pour caramel mixture over your chilled biscuit base.
- Leave in the fridge for 2 hours to set.
- Melt the chocolate in a bowl over a pan of simmering water and pour over the set caramel.
- Leave overnight in the fridge if possible to set.
- Slice into squares and hide the edges for yourself.

Top tip: If you fancy making this for adults just add 200ml of espresso instead of hot chocolate.

Love tiramisu

This is such a lovely bake together treat for kids. For Valentine's Day, we have added hot chocolate instead of coffee to make it more kiddy-friendly.

INGREDIENTS

16 lady fingers (also known as boudoir or savoiardi biscuits)
200ml hot chocolate, made with milk and hot chocolate powder
250g mascarpone
250ml double cream
125g raspberries
2 tbsp icing sugar
1 tsp vanilla essence
40g good-quality chocolate

METHOD

- Put the cream, mascarpone, vanilla essence and icing sugar into a large bowl and whisk until you have the consistency of whipped cream.
- Lay out the lady fingers in a shallow dish then pour the hot chocolate over them so they are nicely soaked but not too soggy.
- Once they are ready, take four serving glasses and put two lady fingers at the bottom of each. Scatter with raspberries and top with your mascarpone mixture.
- Repeat this step to give a nice layered effect, finishing with a layer of the mascarpone cream.
- Dust each one with a little cocoa powder and, for an extra flourish, grate some chocolate on top. Finish off with a raspberry.
- Chill for an hour before serving.

Easy fridge bake sale tray

Having a bake sale in the school and panicking about what to make? I have your back. This easy fridge bake sale tray is just that – easy! And delicious too.

INGREDIENTS
60g unsalted butter
240ml sweetened
    condensed milk
200g milk chocolate
200g digestive biscuits
200g Maltesers

For the topping
200g milk chocolate
Your favourite chocolate
    – we like Kinder
    Bueno and even more
    Maltesers

Top tip: Hide it from the kids before the bake sale or it will be gone!

METHOD

- Line a 20cm square baking tin with baking parchment.
- Crush biscuits and add Maltesers to the crushed biscuits.
- Melt the chocolate. You can do this in the microwave or on the hob in a bowl sitting over a saucepan of simmering water. (Just make sure the bowl isn't sitting in the water.)
- Melt butter and mix together with the chocolate until combined.
- Add to the bowl with the Maltesers and crushed biscuits and mix again.
- Pour over condensed milk and mix again.
- Add to the lined tin and leave to cool.
- Then place in the fridge for at least 3 hours.
- For the topping melt the other bar of chocolate and pour over the top of your cake, reserving some to drizzle on top. Finish by adding squares of your favourite chocolate (we love Kinder Bueno) and more Maltesers.

Homemade fudge

A recipe with three ingredients that tastes amazing that you basically just melt together! Once sliced, add to little airtight jars to make a great present for loved ones.

INGREDIENTS

200g milk chocolate
200g dark chocolate
1 x 397g tin sweetened
   condensed milk

Top tip: Add a few drops of peppermint or vanilla essence for another flavour option.

METHOD

- Add the chocolates to a large mixing bowl with the condensed milk and slowly melt together over a saucepan of simmering water (making sure the bowl doesn't touch the water), keeping your heat low and melting slow.
- You can also add pecan nuts, raisins or a few drops of vanilla essence to mix it up a bit.
- Also don't forget to add a sprinkle of love.
- When all the ingredients have combined and melted together, pour into a 9-inch square tin lined with greaseproof paper.
- Let it cool and place into the fridge overnight to set.
- Slice into small rectangles.

Halloween witches' hats

A super-easy Halloween treat if you fancy making something spooky with the smallies for some Halloween fun.

INGREDIENTS

1 pack of 6 ice-cream cones
1 x 300g pack of rich tea biscuits
2 x 200g bars of chocolate
1 x 200g pack of jelly babies (or your favourite small treats; Smarties are good too)
Sprinkles

METHOD

- Get the kids to break up the chocolate and melt it in a bowl over a pan of simmering water.
- Chop up the treats (or tricks), and get the kids to pop them inside the ice-cream cones.
- Place each ice-cream cone on top of a rich tea biscuit, gluing them together with melted chocolate.
- Brush the whole cone with the melted chocolate (see if the kids can try not to get any in their mouths).
- Finish with sprinkles.
- Leave for about an hour to set.

Top tip: If you are having a Halloween party and feeling brave, you could add some tricks to some of the witches' hats, like pickled onions. See who gets the tricks and who gets the treats!

Top tip: Add 15g of coco to your buttercream to make it chocolatey.

Buttercream cupcakes

One of my very favourite cooking utensils is the wooden spoon. I firmly believe all you really need is a bit of elbow grease and my trusty spoon to make the perfect buttercream cupcakes.

INGREDIENTS

120g self-raising flour
100g butter, softened
100g caster sugar
2 fresh free-range eggs
1 tsp vanilla essence

For the buttercream
100g unsalted butter, softened
200g icing sugar, sifted
1 tsp vanilla essence

Strawberry jam (optional)

METHOD

- Preheat oven to 180°C fan. Prepare a bun tray with bun cases.
- In a large mixing bowl mix together butter, sugar, egg and sifted flour with a wooden spoon to make your batter. Add in the vanilla essence.
- Fill each bun case with a tablespoon of batter.
- Bake for 15–20 minutes until cooked and golden brown.
- Leave to cool while you make your buttercream: in a large bowl add softened butter, sift in the icing sugar and add a teaspoon of vanilla essence.
- Mix together with your wooden spoon until soft and combined.
- With a sharp knife make a hole in the top centre of each bun, saving the cut-out piece. Cut that in half to make butterfly wings.
- Fill each hole with buttercream and a teaspoon of jam.

Raspberry and white chocolate loaf

So this is the perfect little occasion cake for any family party. No matter who we make it for, Lils always decorates it with love and it always goes down a treat.

INGREDIENTS

200g raspberries
200g white chocolate
220g self-raising flour

200g butter, softened
200g caster sugar
3 fresh free-range eggs
1 tsp vanilla essence

Top tip: Dark chocolate works really well too.

METHOD

- Preheat the oven to 180°C fan and line a 2lb loaf tin with parchment paper.
- In a large mixing bowl cream together the butter and sugar with an electric hand whisk.
- Crack in the eggs and whisk together. Drizzle in the vanilla essence.
- Sift in the flour and give another mix.
- Coat your raspberries in a little flour (this stops them from sinking to the bottom), and fold them into the batter with a silicone spatula.
- Add half your batter to the lined loaf tin and add around 6 squares of white chocolate in a little line (keeping the rest to drizzle on top).
- Pour the rest of your batter into the loaf tin on top of the chocolate squares, and bake for 40–50 minutes.
- Insert a skewer into the cooked loaf. If it is cooked through the skewer will come out clean. If there is still batter on the skewer, cook for a few minutes longer.
- Once cooked, leave to cool completely in the tin.
- Melt the rest of the white chocolate in the microwave or on the hob in a bowl over some simmering water.
- When the cake is cooled, decorate by drizzling over white chocolate and adding raspberries on top.

The most important rule for getting kids into the kitchen is not to take it too seriously and have fun! Your cooking creations may not be Pinterest perfect, and the kitchen is going to get messy, but just think of those new cooking skills and magic memories.
Photo credit goes to Simon Walsh.

Temperature and Slow Cooker Conversion Charts

Oven Temperature Conversion Table

Gas	°F	°C	Fan
1	275	140	120
2	300	150	130
3	325	170	150
4	350	180	160
5	375	190	170
6	400	200	180
7	425	220	200
8	450	230	210
9	475	240	220

Slow Cooker Conversion Table

Oven Time	Slow Cooker High	Slow Cooker Low
15–30 minutes	1–2 hours	4–6 hours
30–60 minutes	2–3 hours	5–7 hours
1–2 hours	3–4 hours	6–8 hours
2–4 hours	4–6 hours	8–12 hours

Notes